What to Do...
when what you say isn't working!

SPC Press, Inc.
Knoxville, Tennessee

What to Do...
when what you say isn't working!

Robert Wubbolding, Ed.D.

SPC Press, Inc.
Knoxville, Tennessee

ISBN 0-945320-48-5

2 3 4 5 6 7 8 9

Table of Contents

Dedication

To all people who call themselves
employers,
managers,
supervisors,
or workers.

Acknowledgments

William Glasser, M.D. is the father of the ideas in this book. He developed the method of counseling called Reality Therapy. It is a no-nonsense method of helping people take charge of their lives. He has been, for me, a mentor, a friend, a confidant, and an encourager. To him and to his wife, Carleen, a thousand thank yous!

His contributions to the field of interpersonal relations extend across the planet. I will be grateful if this extension of those important principles lightens the burden of anyone in the work places of the world.

Preface

In this book you will discover what truly motivates all people. You will realize that people have within them a highly efficient "here and now" engine that energizes them to act. The manager's job is to hold a mirror before the employees and ask them to observe themselves. This is accomplished by a delivery system that is immediately usable, down-to-earth, and results-centered—yet humane and empathic. This delivery system is derived from a practical system of counseling known as Reality Therapy which was founded by William Glasser, M.D. I have applied his ideas to coaching employees, but without therapeutic overtones.

The system is summarized by the acronym "W D E P." Each of the letters stands for a cluster of ideas and skills that are explained in detail throughout the book. We call this the WDEP System.

W   **What do you *Want*?**

Explore employees' wants and perceptions: what they want from the job; from themselves. What their viewpoint is of the current situation—and how to improve it.

D   **What are you *Doing*?**

Ask them to look at their own behavior, describing exactly what they are doing.

E   ***Evaluate* what you are doing.**

Have them evaluate their wants, their actions, their willingness to be productive workers. How are their behaviors helping them get what they want? This is the most easily skipped component of the system. It is also the most important one to accomplish

P   **Make a *Plan*.**

Assist them to plan more realistically and precisely to get what they want and to fulfill the wants (mission) of the organization.

The format of this book includes:

- an overview of human motivation;
- ideas that effective managers need to abandon if this system is to work for them;
- what can be gained from using the system;
- the system itself;
- the wrong way and the right way to manage a wide range of specific situations.

I suggest that after reading this book, you put the ideas to work immediately. They are applicable not only at work, but at home. In fact, the most *personal* satisfaction you may gain may be from asking your children the questions from the WDEP System.

But the main focus of this book is on work behaviors. The ideas described bring W. Edward Deming's famous "chain reaction" into the coaching arena. Quality is improved when workers are coached effectively. When they evaluate their own behavior there is less rework and fewer delays. Productivity increases because it is connected with "joy of work." The product cost is lower, the company flourishes, and more jobs are provided.

Effective coaching is thus an attempt to help managers connect with the inner worker—where genuine motivation begins and ends.

Introduction

My writing style in this book is intentionally terse and simple. As you read it, I suggest the following steps.

1. Read the entire book in one or two sessions and mark the chapters and cases that seem relevant to you.

2. Reread the cases you marked and select the one that is most relevant to you.

3. The third step has two parts which can be done immediately after you complete the book.

A. Ask a colleague to read the same chapter or the same case that was most relevant to you. Then discuss it with him or her.

B. Talk to an employee, using the same principles that you read about and discussed. But don't select the most difficult employee in your office or plant. Start with a person who is fairly easy to work with. After you have become comfortable with the ideas, move to the final step.

4. Use the ideas with all employees—and at home with your own children.

***

The cases described in this book should be seen as typical. They represent types of people you deal with every day. You have employees who are similar to (but probably not exactly like) the ones described here. Such employees can often be helped to become more productive. Though you won't be able to make your work place perfect, you can make it better. If you made it 7% to 10% better, you would have a vastly improved organization. If 7% to 10% does not sound impressive, please check with your accountant. Even a seemingly "small difference" can make a major contribution to the company.

Another characteristic of my writing style is the attempt to use language that is non-sexist. Though this sometimes results in the repetition of proper names, I have chosen this style rather than succumb to the exclusivity implied by "he" or "his," etc. On the other hand, I have tried to minimize the use of cumbersome phrases such as "he/she," "his/her," etc. These have been used only when necessary. Also, the proper names used in the cases—Pat, Leslie, Lee, Fran, Lynn, Dale and Jody—have been selected because they can refer to either male or female. The effort to write in such a manner reflects not only the desire for fairness and equality of opportunity, but it also serves to emphasize that the WDEP System is applicable to all persons. For there is more about human nature that unites us than divides us. We all need to evaluate our behavior; we all need to formulate plans to fulfill our inner wants and needs.

Chapter One

Why Employees Succeed or Fail

Motivated employees succeed in their work. There-fore, all managers and supervisors—to some extent—seek to motivate workers. If their efforts to motivate fail, some managers move on to create an atmosphere of fear and coer-cion in which workers may subvert the goals of the organi-zation and provide low quality products or services. A com-mon mistake is the failure to understand that people develop values and motivation from within themselves—not from external forces.

This chapter describes human motivators and the dif-ferences between internal and external controls. A discus-sion on Control Theory follows, including a section on how to tap into the human needs in order to help people find their inner motivation.

I wish I could *make* you feel good about managing and supervising. I wish this book could *make* you a good manager who is seen by your employees as knowledgeable, competent, humane, and in charge of situations. I wish I could *make* you make your employees become dedicated, self-initiating, responsible, prompt, free of interpersonal conflict; people who leave their problems at home. I wish this book could *make* them such! And I wish it could be done instantly—or at least quickly. But that is impossible.

Still, there is a widespread misconception that one person can, somehow, provide a compelling stimulus which causes another person to do something. This erroneous thinking permeates our institutions. Politicians accept it when they believe that stiffer penalties will, of themselves, cure the drug problem. School Boards and Administrators belie this mentality when they waste time seeking more effective punishments with which to control students. Psychologists and others attempt to extinguish, reinforce, and reward behaviors. The world of employment, in which most people spend a high percentage of their time, has surpassed other institutions in affirming the fallacious theory that people can be controlled from above.

Described in this book are ideas that are based upon the belief that employees can be *helped* to be more productive, to feel increased self-esteem, to show initiative, and to do quality work. This is possible only if their needs are met by their work and by the supervising/managing they receive.

So this book is for managers, supervisors, and employers who want to learn how to improve their skills in order to be better coaches for their employees. It is for you—if you are willing to make a real commitment to look fearlessly at your own behavior with a view to changing it for the better. Remember that no person or book can *make* you do anything.

If you make the necessary commitment, you will gain practical, usable, specific skills and ideas. If you have ever supervised or managed an employee who had a case of apathy, resistance, smugness, superiority, boredom, or resentment, you will learn specific ways to talk to such a person.

If you have ever found yourself without words to respond to an employee, or getting defensive, or giving in to the urge to criticize or even verbally attack an employee, you will benefit from implementing the ideas contained in this book. Positive results depend on one condition—*you must put these ideas into practice.* Then you will feel more skillful. Then you will feel more comfortable about your job. You might even look forward to Monday mornings! Your own self-esteem will increase. These are the goals of the coaching method explained in this book. We call it the WDEP System.

Human Motivators

When the inner sources of human motivation are satisfied on the job, the worker feels the "joy in work" described by W. Edwards Deming. These innate needs underlie the behavior of all workers. The needs are *generic* in that they are not specific to any one person or situation. They are *innate* in that they are not learned. They are part of us as we are born and are perhaps present even before birth.

In my training seminars I ask the participants a very important question. "What do you like about your work?" Below is a typical list from one such program. They are listed randomly.

- The people I work with   _____
- Friday at 5:00 PM   _____
- My co-workers   _____
- No two days are alike   _____
- Solving problems   _____
- My best friends are at work   _____
- I can make decisions   _____
- Celebrating after getting a contract   _____
- Working independently   _____
- The confidence others have in me   _____
- The latitude to do what I want   _____
- The paycheck   _____
- Making an impact   _____
- Seeing completion of a project   _____
- Freedom   _____

- Working as a team   _____

- I'm always learning   _____

- I can work without interruptions   _____

- When I didn't make a mistake   _____

- When I'm finished with a report
  and can set it aside   _____

Whether or not the participants realized it, they were discussing their needs; relating their daily work behavior to innate motivational forces. When managers come to deeper knowledge of their own motivation and that of others, they learn that creating the right atmosphere and using the WDEP System makes life more pleasant for everyone. And that, of course, helps make the organization a success.

The conventional method for dealing with employees is based on the theory of external reward and punishment: give people enough incentives, or hold their feet to the fire, and they will become motivated to succeed, to perform, and to contribute to the success of the organization.

This book describes a completely different system of motivation, based on the belief that human beings perform at a higher or lower level of quality because of *internal motivation*—not *external* rewards or punishment.

External Controls Versus Inner Motivation

To use the ideas presented in this book, it is necessary to recognize the difference between *external controls* and *in-*

ner motivation. Human beings are driven to choose behavior, not by externals, but by their own inner ideas of what satisfies them.

As a college student I took a summer job for a steel fabrication company. My job was to grind smooth the welds which the skilled welders executed. The job required that I wear a welder's mask and work in virtual isolation for eight hours a day. The pay was enormous. The supervisor said that I could quickly become a welder because I was a very hard worker. I lasted three weeks on this job. The external reward of salary did not compensate for the pain of working in isolation. In subsequent years, I became a teacher, a counselor, a manager, a promoter, a political campaigner, and an organizer—always working with people.

After reading this chapter, it will be clear that choosing to change jobs, or to perform at any level, is based on the aforementioned "joy in work." Additionally, this chapter explains why people experience joy, satisfaction, and fulfillment in their work as well as the opposites: dislike for their work, resentment toward other people, or apathy toward their own performance.

The Human Brain as a Control System

The WDEP System is based on a system of motivation called *Control Theory.* To adopt this way of thinking, it is useful to understand the analogy of the thermostat. It functions as a control system. In a sense, it has the *desire* to keep the room at a certain temperature. So it attempts to maneuver or control its environment, i.e., the atmosphere in the room. But the thermostat actually has little direct control over the room temperature. All it does have direct control over is its own behavior—the signal it sends to the air conditioning or heating unit.

By analogy, the human brain is similar, emphasizing the following principles.

1. Motivation comes from within. Managers have influence, but force, coercion, or external controls are useless as lasting motivators.

2. Human beings can control only their own behavior. Managers can set an appropriate atmosphere, develop their own coaching skills, and use the WDEP System. Conventional rewards and punishments may control employees for a short time, but being external, they are ineffective in the long run. They do not result in inner need satisfaction and "joy in work."

Several years ago, the CEO of one large company announced to the stockholders that even if they doubled employee salaries, the quality of the product would not increase —not even a tiny bit. Quality would increase only when the employees felt inner pride in their work.

What are the five inner motivators which need to be satisfied in order for a worker to feel joy in work and to be an effective and contributing employee? They are described in this chapter.

Survival, Physical Needs

We are born with the need to preserve our lives. Related to this are such needs as nourishment, shelter, and oxygen. Most managers do not deal with survival needs, but social workers and counselors may often deal with them.

Belonging

Human beings innately seek involvement with others. Infants cannot survive without parents and as children grow, parents become increasingly aware of the importance of friends to every child. The source of many human actions is the need to belong. Anyone with a high need for involvement with people would do better selling a product than working in isolation behind a mask. Workers, young and old, also feel this need to connect with others. Managers using the WDEP System help employees learn to feel a connection with the organization.

Power or Achievement

A sense of accomplishment, or feeling "in control," is an implicit (and sometimes explicit) human motivator. Completing projects, making sales, finding files—all help to fulfill this need. Knowledge, leadership, recognition, and self-esteem are also related to this need.

Enjoyment or Fun

The effective manager helps employees to enjoy their work as much as possible. Laughing is a behavior that belongs exclusively to human beings. Aristotle said that the essence of being human, rather than animal, is the ability to laugh. Work that is mindless and boring—that holds no joy —is dehumanizing in a profound way.

Freedom or Independence

No one enjoys coercion. We all like to choose. An effective parent helps the child learn the importance of making choices and taking responsibility for the consequences. Similarly, the manager encourages employees to examine their choices, allowing as much freedom and independence as is reasonably possible.

An Exercise in Applying the Need System

In order to connect specific activities to the needs motivation system, return to the list of likes on pages 4–5: Survival, Belonging, Power/Achievement, Enjoyment/Fun, and Freedom. Label the need that is fulfilled by each one. Some answers are obvious. For instance, liking people at work clearly relates to belonging. Others are more ambiguous and may relate to several needs. The value of this exercise is thinking about how to relate needs to behaviors. It would also be helpful to discuss the exercise with others.

A seminar participant questioned, "Is it realistic to be able to fulfill all these needs and wants at work?" The answer is no. It is not possible to fulfill all the needs, all the time, on the job. But workers doing quality work, maintaining interest in the job, and avoiding burnout are able to meet their needs to some extent. Not every aspect of a job involves complete satisfaction. But when work responsibilities provide at least a modicum of belonging, power, fun, and freedom, productive behavior of employees is evident.

Characteristics of the Needs

- *Innate*

  The needs are in-born. We arrive in the world with the needs immediately beginning to generate behaviors.

- *Universal*

  They are not limited to any one culture, sex, race, or geographical location.

- *General*

  The needs are not specific. No one has an intrinsic need for a job, money, etc. The need is for something more fundamental: accomplishment, achievement, a sense of being in control of one's life.

- *Conflictual*

  Sometimes the fulfillment of one need might interfere with the fulfillment of another, i.e., the attainment of fun might interfere with satisfying the need for power. Or the fulfillment of one's need might interfere with the fulfillment of another's. (A gathering at the water fountain often interferes with the manager's need for power —especially if the latter is not the one who is thirsty!)

The Inner Quality World

Human beings are motivated to make choices, first and foremost, according to the human needs: belonging, power or achievement, fun or enjoyment, and freedom or independence. *But more specifically,* each person builds an inner world of specific wants, unique to themselves, but related to people, work, leisure, etc. This inner world of wants ranges from major goals to minor desires. It defines "quality" for each person—the "quality world" of each worker.

Workers want to feel in control of their destiny; to feel that their work is important; to enjoy the work and avoid boredom. They generally like to feel they can make decisions. This accounts for the effectiveness of quality circles in which workers' ideas are implemented and they do not feel manipulated by management.

An effective manager understands how to infuse quality job performance into the employee's own quality world. This is accomplished by using the WDEP System—

- Determine their *Wants*
- Describe what is being *Done*
- *Evaluate* a Specific Behavior and/or the attainability of their Want
- Make a Specific, Realistic *Plan*

In summary, human beings are motivated from the inside—to fulfill their general needs and their specific wants—

which on the job, transfers to their "quality worlds." The effective manager taps into this inner motivation and helps them feel joy in work by using the delivery system described in detail in this book—the WDEP System.

Chapter Two

The Current Scene

Current managerial practice and theory are brimming over with assumptions and philosophies that, in reality, are counterproductive to the effective management of people. While these are rarely accepted and articulated explicitly, they nevertheless underlie specific supervisory and managerial behaviors.

Ideas to Absolutely Give Up

The four ideas summarized in this section are ineffective and actually constitute barriers to increased quality. To use the ideas and skills described in this book, you must decide to abandon, surrender, give up, abolish, and mentally banish these four fallacious ideas!

1. As a manager, I can force the employees to do what I want them to do.

Some managers relentlessly and unswervingly cling to the misguided belief that they can control employees with rewards and coercion. They naively believe that the right kind of "prod" will make people perform more effectively. During the Great Depression years, many managers virtually did have the power of life or death over employees. Now however, even with the constant threat of corporate down-sizing, managers must use interpersonal and relational skills to motivate employees. The old motto—my way or the highway—no longer works. Today there are few threats which are sufficient to induce some people to change what they do—much less what they think. And even reward systems are suspect as effective motivators.

2. Increasing the compensation package is sufficient to keep people happy.

This mistaken belief is similar to the previous one and is an application of it. Although money is an important desire in the minds of many people, human motivation is complex and variegated. What motivates one person does not necessarily motivate others.

That employees will have a salary is a given. With that assumption, their moment-to-moment motivation comes from the five inner needs. They want and need more than the salary. The "more" may be monetary, but more often it involves other forms of need fulfillment.

3. It is not necessary to reward people for "doing what they are supposed to do."

This philosophy fails to account for the human needs that drive behavior. In a previous age, when people accepted more control from authority, this mind-set might have been effective. But since the 1950s it has created rebellion and resistance on the part of workers. The desire to act independently can be squelched for a while. In fact, entire nations have enforced it for years. But the social upheaval and economic disasters of the late 1980s bore witness to the irrepressible desire of people to be free from dictatorial, unappreciative management.

4. People are good, honest, and will always perform to the best of their ability.

On the contrary, people are human, fallible, and prone to make mistakes. We misconstrue, misinterpret, and mislead. We can beguile and bedazzle. We can work at cross purposes, make blunders, and get lost in trivialities. Illogic, indefiniteness, and ill-advice can all be seen in human behavior. We can even be delusive, deriding, deceitful, if not downright demonic. In short, Murphy was an optimist!

***

The neophyte (or idealistic) manager or supervisor quickly discovers that whatever the problem may appear to be, at its root is a "people problem." One study showed that the ability of companies to make a profit depended 87% on people skills and only 13% on technical skills.

This book is an attempt to help supervisors, foremen, and managers deal realistically with employees without becoming cynical or bitter; without either withdrawing from subordinates or "hammering" on them in a sarcastic way. It provides solid, down-to-earth skills that can be used in any setting.

Managerial Styles

The traditional way to look at leadership and management is to categorize behaviors under three styles: Authoritarian, Laissez-faire, and Participatory (or Democratic).

Authoritarian Management

Authoritarian Managers, sometimes called "Boss Managers" by William Glasser, view accountability as the greatest invention of the twentieth century. They emphasize the element of *firmness* which they hear in the WDEP System. People under them are treated like computers: given commands and expected to carry them out unquestioningly. It has become chic to label this style as worthless—but it is not always ineffective or inappropriate. It is only the extreme autocratic style that should be completely rejected.

The Authoritarian Manager's sole objective is to maintain his/her own position. Perhaps it was this type of manager that Seneca had in mind when he said, "The aim of power is to maintain power." Such a leader hoards information, using it to manipulate employees into conformity. Authoritarian Managers rule by whimsy, ignoring the wants and needs of others. At any cost, the Authoritarian Manager seeks to be "King (Queen) of the Hill" and to retain superiority through a rule of fear. People are not seen as helpful partners, but as threats to the autocrat's power.

A related managerial style is Authoritarian, but Humane. Such a leader is clear, consistent, and fair. These managers are less inclined to ask about the wants or needs of others because they think they already know what is needed. Information to subordinates is provided only when asked or on a "need to know" basis.

This manager has good instincts and is often quite charismatic. I once had an employer who was said to run "the tightest ship in the Navy." Many employees shivered when he approached, but they would also take any hill for him. As one worker said, "If Larry says it's going to rain, you can set your tubs out."

Military commanders use the Authoritarian Style when they shout, "Take the hill!" They often do not claim credit for capturing the hill. On the contrary, they are frequently willing to give credit to others because they have no personal vested interest in owning the hill.

Sometimes, such as in war, authoritarian decisions are frequent and necessary. When the sergeant says, "Take the hill!" there is little opportunity to discuss it in a democratic way. But transferring this "take the hill" mentality to the civilian world of business, civil service, plant management, or governmental agency, can only result in unhappiness, misery, and increased pugnacity on the part of both worker and managers.

The Authoritarian Management Style described here could include a watered-down use of the WDEP System. The limitation of this style is that such managers use the system to a slight degree but fail to ask questions of their subordinates. Failing to see workers as colleagues or collaborators, they decide what will get the job done without attention to the wants, perceptions, or opinions of others. They seek no input. They make the evaluations themselves and formulate plans—imposing them from above.

The Authoritarian Manager's time has long passed, but many managers still naively cling to the belief that they can force others to conform to blindly-imposed standards. While there is a place for the issuance of orders, autocracy no longer works effectively in the day-to-day administration of modern companies or organizations.

Laissez-faire Management

The second major type of management is that of Laissez-faire, or "Management by Withdrawal." This manager allows events to take their natural course. Such a person delegates work, authority, and responsibility. Worst of all, instead of setting standards of quality, he/she delegates that task to others (who may well decide that their own behaviors are the highest standards of achievable quality).

Characteristics of the Laissez-faire Manager includes an excessive desire to belong and to be liked. They frequently fear to exercise power, and this timidity is often illustrated by a feeble attempt to show leadership.

But when the employees cannot be manipulated by the people-pleasing or withdrawal behaviors, the leader often becomes disillusioned, cynical, and bitter toward the employees. Such managers fail to see that although employees are fallible, they also have needs and wants and can be motivated if they are dealt with by using the WDEP System.

Often this "let it happen" mentality results in disaster, and the Laissez-faire Manager then resorts to an authoritarian approach, bitterly believing that people cannot be trusted. As one such manager said, "I tried being a nice guy and allowing people to be on their own. But when they screwed up so much, I changed. Now, I watch their every damn move." The person's tone, as well as the content of the statement indicated that participatory management was not the style that was adopted.

Unless or until the above extreme has been reached, the Laissez-faire Manager would allow subordinates to use the WDEP System. And this style of leadership can work quite well with people who are extremely conscientious or are held accountable in alternative ways. For example, university administrators rarely conduct close supervision of a university instructor's classes or hours. If the classes do not meet the students' needs, they usually let the instructor know. Obviously there are advantages and disadvantages to this style. It provides space for the self-initiator as well as for the indolent employee.

Participatory (or Democratic) Management

The third type of management is more democratic and involves varying degrees of participation. William Glasser refers to this style as "Lead Management." The Participatory Manager seeks to involve others as decision makers. The leader recognizes that all workers are motivated by needs that must be fulfilled in a satisfactory way within the context of their jobs.

The WDEP System is most appropriately used in Participatory Management. This manager seeks input before making decisions. The expression of wants by subordinates, who are seen as collaborators, is allowed and encouraged. Decisions made with input from others are viewed by the Participatory Manager as necessary and useful—not merely as unavoidable. Therefore, they recognize that lip service to these principles is not enough. Rather, they seek to establish and consistently use specific structures designed to secure the involvement of many people.

This book explains how the Participatory (or Democratic) Manager can utilize the WDEP System to increase the quality of service and products, while helping employees meet their needs through their work.

Chapter Three

What to Expect...

The WDEP System of Conferencing and Coaching

Think Back...

You are a supervisor or manager because you succeeded in your work. You probably had positive attitudes and qualities when you started. Think of your first enjoyable job. Do you remember your enthusiasm—the *honeymoon* period? You were excited and thought, "This is for me. I'm doing something worthwhile. I feel good about my job and about myself."

You've probably passed your first rush of joy in work, and you may never recapture that first fervor. But you may be able to move forward toward a renewed enthusiasm—perhaps even excitement—about your work.

At this point, you can understand that the reason you felt good and felt successful is that you were doing something which you were proud of; which satisfied something inside of you. You were good at your job. You believed that you had the talent and the skill to succeed. Now, you may feel "stuck"—or even burned out. But if you raise your skills to a new and higher level, you can regain some of your previous enthusiasm. To become a more successful manager requires that you develop a new set of skills.

Consider—making a widget requires a definite skill. Selling it requires other skills. And motivating others to commit to a high quality product requires even different skills. These motivational skills are what this book teaches.

The effective manager must be able to conduct personal and group conferences which are more than cheerleading; free of criticism, devoid of preaching, and which go far beyond bestowing rewards and punishments. The use of the WDEP System will help you elicit commitment and enhance the quality of the products or services of your organization.

In order to use this system, you must realize that we all make mistakes in managing employees. The next few chapters describe these mistakes and what to do about them.

Preparing for Desired Outcomes

The WDEP System will provide you with skills for dealing with employees who:

- are tardy for work,

- argue with co-workers,

- lack initiative,

- perform below their potential,

- fail to follow through,

- are not assertive,

- are aggressive toward others,

- choose not to follow instructions,

- seem to be moody,

- bring their personal problems into the office,

- do poor quality work,

- do not show necessary leadership,

- fail to communicate effectively,

- gripe excessively,

- are overly agreeable, and

- hide their own good ideas.

In order to prepare your mind to receive the ideas contained in these chapters, write a description on the next page of two employees with whom you need help. Try to be specific in describing their behavior.

When you finish reading this book, return to these cases and create your own scenario for each of them, including your questions and statements as well as theirs.

Employee # 1 – Description of his/her behavior:

_____

_____

_____

_____

_____

_____

Employee # 2 – Description of his/her behavior:

_____

_____

_____

_____

_____

_____

Now re-read the cases you've written about. Be sure you have not just identified people, but have described their specific behaviors.

Chapter Four

The WDEP System: What Is It?

If you have read this far, I will assume you have made a mental commitment to continue and are willing to learn the WDEP System which is summarized in this chapter.

Each of the letters...

W

D

E

P

...stands for a cluster of questions to be explored with employees while coaching, counseling, supervising, and motivating them.

This system of coaching employees taps into the inner needs of workers. It provides specific questions for the manager to ask, and these questions elicit a higher level of motivation. The workers define specific *wants* (**W**) related to needs. They examine what they are *doing* (**D**). Most importantly, they *evaluate* (**E**) the attainability of their wants, as well as the helpfulness of their own actions. Finally, they make specific, attainable *plans* (**P**).

The effective use of this system enables the manager to put responsibility directly on the employee, avoid excuses, deal humanely with the workers, and create an atmosphere in which people feel more dedicated to the quality of their work.

W = WANTS

Explore the *wants* of the employees. Ask them what they want from their jobs, from their co-workers, from themselves, and from you—the manager or coach. Human wants are an outgrowth of the human needs. Consequently, workers always want things specifically related to their needs, including such things as friendly relationships, job satisfaction, a sense of accomplishment, a job that is enjoyable, and at least some latitude in performing their job. If these wants are fulfilled, they will have the "joy in work" described by Dr. Deming.

First, I especially suggest that you ask people what they want from their jobs. Is the job satisfying to them? What frustrates them? Where do they want to be now... in a year... in five years...?

Employees generally have a difficult time answering these questions. Because they have not been asked such questions very often, they will not always be able to define their wants clearly and precisely. Therefore, the manager needs to make such inquiries often. Moreover, *wants* are continually changing. What is desirable to an employee today might not be appealing a week, a month, or six months from now. And finally, they should be asked which of their *wants* they are, and are not, getting.

A most valuable question is, "How strongly do you want it?" (referring to a job, promotion, increase in salary, etc.). Keep in mind that there are several levels of commitment to quality. The supervisor should gradually nudge the employee toward each higher level. The levels, as described by workers, are:

Level One
"I don't care. I hate it here. Don't bother me."

This is the lowest level of commitment. In fact, it is *no commitment* at all. Such an employee is in dire need of effective WDEP managing.

Level Two
"I don't know what I want."

Such people have only a vague idea of what the world of work has to offer them. They need help in clarifying their goals. Their work is usually passable, but they require more supervision than you might be able or willing to provide.

Level Three
"I want something better for myself."

These employees want to move up to a promotion, more responsibility, or increased salary, and are fairly good workers. But they may not understand that quality work and "going the extra mile" is the way to achieve these goals.

Level Four
*"I have a specific goal for myself
and I'm willing to work hard to attain it."*

Such employees take initiative, follow through, and are easy to work with. Managers do not want to see them transferred to other departments.

Level Five
*"I have a burning desire to contribute
to the maximum of my ability
so that I will be an invaluable employee
because my work is of the highest quality—
the minimum which I choose to settle for."*

This is the high flyer—the future company president!

***

Each level is higher than the previous one. Managers can feel successful when they are able to lead people to higher levels; to help an employee become even a little more committed to higher quality or to small increases in positive motivation. These increases are stepping stones to even higher levels of commitment and increased quality of product and service.

D = DOING AND DIRECTION

Explore where the employees' behavior is leading them. Talk about their overall direction, but also be specific about recent, specific actions. If they have habitually poor attendance, ask them where their tardiness or absenteeism is leading them. If they socialize too much, ask them where chatting for 45 minutes a day is taking them. Explore specific incidents or parts of a workday in a detailed manner.

This comprises one half of the "mirror technique." (The Evaluation component, explained below, is the second half of this technique.) It is as though you are holding a mirror before them and asking them to look at it and tell you exactly what they see. This works much better than pointing a finger and accusing them of being irresponsible. Your questions help them to look at themselves and see aspects of their behavior that they hadn't thought of previously. The key for the manager is two-fold.

- Your questions must be specific and exact.
- You must be non-critical. Employees will often be defensive anyway, but blaming will result in added resistance to you as manager.

E = EVALUATION

This component takes many forms, identifiable by the following series of questions. In this second part of the "mirror technique," employees are asked to go beyond a description of what they see. They are asked to make a judgment or a determination about the effectiveness of their actions and the attainability of their wants. Each question should be about a specific incident or behavior.

1. Is what you want realistic or attainable?

2. Is your action helpful in getting the job done?

3. Is your action helpful to others?

4. Is your action helping you get what you want? (This sounds simple, but the fact is, many people do not connect what they *do* with what they *want.*)

5. Is your action in line with or against the explicit rules of the company? (I'd strongly suggest avoiding the time-worn phrase "company policy," which is usually an instant turn-off. At this remark, employees' eyes usually glaze over and get a far-away look. Their minds often drift away, never to be heard from again!)

6. Is your action acceptable (in line with common sense, even though it might not be against an explicit rule)?

7. Is your action helping the company achieve its goals (provide a high quality product or service to the public, make a profit, and stay in business) so you can maintain a secure job for yourself?

8. Is your plan for improvement attainable and helpful?

Note:

- While reading the dialogues in the book, it is important to remember that they are intended to represent the various components of the WDEP System. Thus they are out of context. In the real world there is a context, i.e., a pre-existing relationship between worker and manager.

- Also remember that the above list contains all the evaluation components. It would be rare for a manager to use all the evaluation components in such a short time or in one interview.

- Finally, a manager who uses this system would also spend time discussing the worker's successes, contributions, and positive behaviors.

***

In the following dialogue, Pat, ordinarily a conscientious middle manager for a large company, has been exhibiting several unacceptable behaviors. The manager asks to have a talk with Pat.

Mgr.   Pat, how are things going?

Pat   I've worked here six months and I would like to be promoted.

Mgr.   We haven't promoted anyone before they've worked nine months. How realistic is it for you to expect a promotion three months early?

Pat   I guess I'll have to wait.

Mgr.   That's right. There are some other things I wanted to talk to you about, Pat. I've noticed that you've been leaving early, and it's also been quite noticeable to people under you.

Pat   Yeah, I guess I have. But I also worked overtime last month.

Mgr.   If you continue to leave early, what effect will it have on the distribution of the work?

Pat   Well...others have to pick up the slack.

Mgr.   How about the effect on the length of time to get the work done?

Pat   It probably takes longer.

Mgr.   Aside from the amount of time, what effect does it have on the people under you when they see you leave early?

Pat   I guess they aren't too impressed when their supervisor sets a bad example for them.

Mgr.   I've also noticed you've been complaining in front of your people. What effect does griping and leaving early have on the promotion you are shooting for?

Pat   I guess it won't help.

Mgr.   What would help you get what you want?

Pat   I need to get back to my old self.

Mgr.   I agree. Also, what about the rules?

Pat   It's pretty clear we're supposed to be here until 4:45...salaried people are not exceptions.

Mgr.   You know, there's no rule about complaining, but what is the impact on other people?

Pat   It takes them down too.

Mgr.   What about the leader's impact on others?

Pat   They'll perform at a lower level if I lower my level of quality.

Mgr.   So what about the future?

Pat   I guess I need to turn around.

Mgr.   Think it would help?

Pat   Of course.

Mgr.   Could you make a plan?

Pat: I guess so.

Mgr.   A firm plan?

Pat   All right. All right. I'll stay till 4:45 from now on.

Mgr.	"From now on" is too long. What would be more realistic?
Pat	I'll do it for two weeks.
Mgr.	What about complaints?
Pat	Yeah, I'll stop.
Mgr.	Maybe just bite your tongue for a few days. Let's talk again in a week or so.

Again, remember that the evaluation component comprises the second part of the "mirror technique" which is composed of two main questions:

1. "What are you doing?"
   (Or perhaps, "What did you do yesterday?")
2. "Did it help?" (Was your behavior effective?)

Using this method of skillful questioning, the evaluation becomes the employee's own evaluation. Managers have their own ideas about effectiveness, but for genuine change to occur, employees need to evaluate for themselves—from the inside.

P = PLANNING

Asking employees "What will you do to improve?" seems to be the easiest component of the WDEP System. However, to be effective this question must be preceded by the other components. When the manager reaches the planning stage, an important look to the future is crucial. "Where do you go from here? What will you do differently today? Will you stay until 4:45? Will you be on time for one week?" And in the case of Pat..."to be on time for two weeks."

An effective plan has at least six characteristics. Desired changes are achieved when the manager helps the employee make plans that we call *"SAMICC" Plans* (Simple, Attainable, Measurable, Immediate, Consistent, and Controlled).

*Simple...*to the point; not complicated. Pat's plan was to be on time and to bite the tongue.

*Attainable...*realistically doable. It should not be overwhelming and unattainable. At first Pat wanted to stay until 4:45 "from now on." The manager suggested that it was more realistic to limit the time frame to two weeks.

*Measurable...*precise, exact, clear. A vague plan "to improve" or "to do better" would not be sufficient. Consider...when you call an airline for a plane ticket, you want to know exactly what time the plane leaves. If the airline agent said to you, "the flight leaves later," you would insist on being given more precise information! Plans made during motivational conferences should be measurable and well defined.

*Immediate...*executed as quickly as possible. There is no need to wait. The effective manager helps the employee to implement the plan today. The prayer of the WDEP Manager is *not* that of St. Augustine... "God give me chastity, but not yet."

*Consistent...*repeated over and over. The plan is not a one-shot deal. It should be repetitive if it is to make a difference. Pat planned to be on time *every* day and to stay until 4:45.

*Controlled...*by the planner—not an "if" plan. An effective plan is based solely on the planner's behavior, not on that of the other employees. Pat's plan to bite the tongue did not depend on what others did. Pat would take the lead and do better regardless of what others did. The plan depended exclusively on Pat's choice.

It is quite useful to suggest a plan. But it is even more useful to begin with the employee's plan. Ask employees if they have thought through their plans. Ask them about other employees who are productive and successful. What do they do to attain their goals and to feel good about their work?

Ultimately the plan must be owned and operated by the worker. Forcing a plan is a tactic of the "Boss Manager," and it rarely works. Good questioning helps the employee formulate and commit to a plan to increase or maintain high quality.

The WDEP System is easy to understand. Nevertheless, it is a skill that needs to be practiced. Thus, this book contains hypothetical transcripts of specific ways to implement this practical, down-to-earth, jargon-free system.

Chapter Five

Building the Environment

The use of the WDEP System does not occur in a vacuum. Its effectiveness rests on the willingness of the manager to adopt the role of coach. A coach sets an atmosphere in which all participants can work together for the benefit of the group. A coach teaches, inspires, and helps the players commit to high-quality behavior. The coach gives the team credit for success. In return, the coach often enjoys the credit bestowed by others.

What to Avoid

Establishing an appropriate environment means avoiding certain destructive choices. The behaviors listed below constitute severe attacks on the employees' needs. They are even more damaging when done in front of others. Consequently, I suggest avoiding them altogether.

Arguing

It serves little purpose to argue with employees about their work habits. Such arguments are power struggles and the mere entrance into the struggle means that the manager has lost.

Belittling

Even an isolated put-down of an employee increases resentment.

Criticizing

Seeing the negative in a person's behavior is sometimes necessary and unavoidable. But the WDEP System helps the manager identify positive behaviors and build on them by helping employees make better choices.

Demeaning

This is a more severe form of belittling—often habitual in nature.

Excusing

It is usually not helpful to dwell on excuses. They occur when a person puts the responsibility for a behavior on external causes. "I'm late because of the traffic," or "The other department didn't do their work so the project is not completed," are examples of the many excuses we make and hear from others. For more about excuses, see the end of the chapter.

Instill Fear

While fear of danger is appropriate, fear is not a motivator for quality performance at work. It lessens efficiency and arouses a competitive instinct in employees. This is destructive to teamwork and quality performance.

Giving Up Easily

Managers are often tempted to give up on an employee. But the effective coach doesn't give up on anyone. On the contrary, persistence and perseverance are characteristics of the WDEP System Manager. Moreover, the manager does not give up on using the components of WDEP System. Some managers want a quick fix to remedy long-term problems or deep-seated habits. But while you should expect to see results, it is important to realize that repeated use of the principles is necessary for long-term results.

What to Do

Besides avoiding the negative behaviors which create a toxic work environment, I suggest that the following positive attitudes and behaviors facilitate a healthy atmosphere.

Courtesy, Determination, Enthusiasm, Firmness

The effective coach chooses a civilized style of coaching employees. Courtesy implies basic respect for the workers who are, after all, usually doing their best at any given moment. But when problems occur, it is the job of the manager to help employees improve their performance.

Determination implies a "we will work it out" viewpoint. If the coach is to be a genuine leader, determination to solve problems and an unwillingness to settle on mediocrity must be evident to all.

Looking for the bright side and building on strengths is not naive, Pollyanna cheerleading. It is *enthusiasm*—and it is necessary if managers are to maintain their proper roles. Thomas Edison once remarked that if we left our children nothing but enthusiasm, they would have a legacy of incalculable value.

Leaders must set standards, make decisions, and utilize consequences. Firmness is a necessary quality. To be democratic is not to be flaccid.

Discussion of Quality

The manager should involve workers in a continuing dialogue about quality: what it is and how it relates to their work.

In his book, *The New Economics*, W. Edwards Deming defines a quality product as one which "helps somebody and enjoys a good and sustainable market." William Glasser says that quality feels good, is useful, and is a person's best effort. I would add that a quality product or service does what it is supposed to do. It lasts, and it satisfies its user. And all agree that quality can always be improved. It is a journey—not a destination. It is a moving target.

Establishment of Trust

Since trust is built on fairness and consistency, managers who discriminate or treat workers unfairly find the WDEP System worthless. Still, treating people fairly does not mean treating each one exactly the same. In their book, *Discipline With Dignity*, Curwin and Mendler state that fairness means dealing with people on the basis of their needs. The physician does not treat all patients' illnesses the same. Each patient is treated differently but according to their physical requirements.

The goals of the above suggestions are indeed lofty. They include facilitating a work atmosphere that allows for and encourages employees to:

- admit mistakes and correct them without fear,
- develop their creativity,
- contribute to the organization,
- and meet their own needs by finding an intrinsic satisfaction in their work, as well as performing at a high level of quality.

You are invited to list on the next page some applications to your own behavior. What can you do better to establish the foundation for the effective use of the WDEP System?

_____

_____

_____

Further Notes on Excuses

As you read the cases in the book, I suggest that you make special note of excuses and how the manager handled them. Also you might spend a few minutes thinking about whether you have heard any of the following statements at home or work and how you have handled them.

"I hit him because he hit me first."

"The dog ate my homework."

"Everybody else is going to the party and will be home late."

"The weather depresses me."

"Other people annoy me."

You are invited to add your own favorite excuses in the spaces below.

_____

_____

_____

Chapter Six

A Word About the Cases

Each case described in this book should be seen as a *distillation*. They are summaries of what might occur over a longer period of time and/or during several sessions. Thus, dialogue not illustrating my main point is viewed as superfluous to the lesson and is, therefore, omitted.

In order to teach in a clear and unambiguous manner, I have purposely made the cases simple and unentangled. Although some of the cases presented as "managerial mistakes" may seem simplistic, they are intended to illustrate behaviors that managers and supervisors may choose for lack of a more effective skill.

I must also emphasize that people might exhibit one or another of these behaviors only on occasion—not habitually.

So even the Authoritarian Manager could exhibit Laissez-faire behavior at a given moment, with a specific person, or about a particular issue. Similarly, the skilled practitioner of the WDEP System could occasionally (and less effectively) resort to autocratic or laissez-faire behaviors. A human being that is 100% consistent is a rarity. In short, even the best leader can sometimes act like a boss (in the worst sense of that particular word).

Parallel to the distilled manner in which all cases are presented is the succinct format used in the description of the WDEP System. I have eliminated ordinary small talk and discussion of side issues that a typical conference would contain. This omission is designed, not to suggest that such talk is inappropriate, but to emphasize the essence of the lesson to be learned.

The information in each case illustrates the use of the WDEP System in focusing on productive employee behaviors. I suspect the reader already knows how to discuss side issues: the recent football game, clothes, children, world problems and their solutions. My goal is to teach you, in a very short space, practical, down-to-earth, and immediately-useful skills.

These skills can be used in the office, plant, agency— and in your home as you valiantly endeavor to supervise and manage your children.

Chapter Seven

Being Overly Nice...
Overly Authoritarian...
And an Alternative

Overly Nice: The Case of Leslie

In this case, Leslie is a good employee who has developed attendance problems. Leslie has been late two days a week on a regular basis, leaves early equally as often, and has lost other time from the job. The Supervisor doesn't want to lose Leslie whose work is usually quite good. The ensuing conversation sounds something like the following.

Sup.   Leslie, you've been late and you've lost a lot of other time too. I need to talk about this with you and see if we can solve the problems.

Leslie   I'm so sorry. I'll try to do better. Things are extra rough for me lately. I don't know how some people do what everything that I have to do every day.

Sup. What seems to be the problem?

Leslie You know I'm a single parent and ever since my spouse left me, it's been rough. I have to do it all now. I don't get any help and the kids take advantage of me.

Sup. It's really hard to do everything by yourself. Tell me about it.

Leslie It is hard. I'm not used to it. Before the divorce, we shared the chores. Now, it's all up to me.

Sup. Is that why you've been late?

Leslie Well today I had to wake Sue about five times. She can't seem to get up because she stays up too late at night. She missed the bus, and I had to drive fast to catch it as it came down another road. And Jimmy needs a big breakfast every day because the coach said he should eat a lot in the morning. So in the last few months, he's insisted on a full meal at 6:30 in the morning. I must say that I've learned to cook breakfast again! Then I have to be sure they have all their books and other projects and are ready to get to the bus stop. If they miss the bus, I usually drive them all the way to school—if I can't catch the bus—and then I get to work even later.

Sup. You have a hard time even before you get here!

Leslie I sure do, and that's not all. Some days it's icy and the car gets stuck and I keep spinning the wheels. You know we live on a dead-end street and they don't salt and sand the street till later in the day, if at all. Have I been late too much when the weather is bad?

Sup. Well, yes, but then a lot of people are late when the roads are bad.

Leslie That's good to know.

Sup. Well...you're later than the others. I know it's been rough. I don't know how you do it. However, my manager is quite upset about tardiness among my

	people so he said I should talk to you about why you're late. But now I understand. Still, you know we like to start at 8:00 am.
Leslie	I know, but I can't get here on time every day.
Sup.	Well...I understand you have a rough time of it.
Leslie	Can't we make an exception? I am a good worker. You've told me that often.
Sup.	Well...you are a good worker and I don't want to lose you. But we don't normally make exceptions.
Leslie	Couldn't we have flex time? They do in several places. It would make it so much easier on a lot of us. You know, they have it at the ABC Company. They all have to be there from 10:00 am till 2:00 pm, but they can work out all their other hours individually.
Sup.	It sure would be a good idea.
Leslie	You bet it would. Do you think you could talk to your manager about this? I'd really appreciate it, and I know the others would, too.
Sup.	I know that management has talked about flex time in the past, but I think they decided against it. I've always liked the idea a lot.
Leslie	Are you sure they won't do it? Could you talk to them again? We'd all love to have it.
Sup.	I'll look into it again, but I'm pretty sure they've made a decision. Still, I'll ask my manager about it. Besides, you have a lot of good reasons for being late and I don't want to lose you.
Leslie	I'm glad you agree.
Sup.	Now tell me why you leave work early so often.
Leslie	Well, that's a different story.
Sup.	Oh? How is it different?
Leslie	I have to car pool the kids. They have soccer and other things. When it's my turn, I don't have any

other choice but to take care of my responsibility. Other people carry their weight and I have to carry mine. Then again, I had to talk to the lawyer about the divorce, and I have to get there on time as it is a big firm and they schedule appointments tightly. I don't want to be late because of traffic. Besides all that, I've had some sickness. Since my divorce, my allergies are acting up and I've been going to the doctor a lot more often.

Sup.   You sure have been through it! I can understand why you've had to leave early. But could you try to keep it to a minimum?

Leslie   I'll try. Will you talk to your manager about flex time, or at least about allowing an exception for me?

Sup.   I'll make an appointment and see what I can do.

In this conference, the supervisor has attempted to be kind and empathic. Often such supervisors have had training in listening skills and they mistakenly believe that listening is the same as solving the problem. This supervisor knew that flex time was not an option, and that no exception could be made. Nevertheless, he/she accepted the responsibility for trying to get it for Leslie.

One of the key statements by Leslie was "We'd all love to have it," (flex time). This Laissez-faire Supervisor, seeking to satisfy a high need for approval, and wanting to be a "nice guy," has made a very ineffective decision that will ultimately result in less approval by his/her manager—as well as by the employees whose false hope will ultimately be dashed. Such conferences serve only to delay facing the problem and dealing with an uncomfortable situation—

namely a good worker who violates one of the command-
ments of the work ethic: "Thou shalt show up every day, on
time, and stay till quitting time."

My prediction for this supervisor is that he/she will go
to the manager and get answers which are already known—
no flex time and no exceptions. The manager might then tell
the supervisor to solve the problem, to avoid becoming an
advocate for employees who break the rules, and to stop
wasting valuable time when the solution is evident. The supervisor will then feel even less self-esteem, more foolish,
and weaker. The supervisor will also feel afraid to confront
Leslie again because Leslie will feel put down. At the end,
our supervisor, who wants to be "nice" will now be seen as
weak—and not so nice after all.

In short, the supervisor who wanted to appear strong
and capable to management now feels the opposite. The supervisor who wanted to be nice to the employee now must
play the role of the ogre.

In the long run, such supervisors loathe conferences
with employees and will do anything to avoid discussions
with them. In reality, it takes a Henry Kissinger to succeed
at this kind of shuttle diplomacy, and most of us are not
Kissingers.

Overly Authoritarian: Leslie Again

Here again, Leslie's supervisor attempts a conference.
But this supervisor has a different belief system. Far from

the permissive, overly sympathetic Laissez-faire Manager, this supervisor is the Authoritarian Manager—with Intolerance as a middle name and the sole aim of being sure that people do what they are supposed to do. This consistently noxious and magisterial style is not unnoticed by Leslie and others, who see the supervisor as unhelpful, unaccommodating, and rigidly uncaring. Their description is simply— "cold." But when the sergeant says, "Take the hill!" the troops take the hill...or do they?

The conversation begins in the same manner as before, but quickly makes a sharp turn:

Sup.   Leslie, you've been late and have lost other time too.

Leslie   I'm so sorry. I'll try to do better. Things are extra rough for me lately. I don't know how some people do what I have to do everyday.

Sup.   See to it now. If you have a problem, fix it.

Leslie   But I'm a single parent. I'm on my own with two kids now that my spouse has left me.

Sup.   Don't burden me with your personal problems. It's company policy to start on time at 8:00 am, not 8:15 or 8:30. We require that you be here at that time and stay until 5:00.

Leslie   But I'm doing the best I can to get here.

Sup.   Then do better. You know the policy. We can't allow exceptions around here or we'll have chaos.

Leslie   But my family prevents me from getting here on time once in a while. Also I need to take care of them in the afternoons. It hasn't been that often anyway.

Sup.   Keep your personal problems out of it. When you come to work, leave them at the door—or better,

leave them at home. We're not running a social
service agency.

Leslie Why are you picking on me? Are you calling in the
others to talk to them, too?

Sup. What's that got to do with it? I'm telling you to take
care of your business, so get to it!

Leslie Okay! I'll try. (Leaves the session in a very bad
mood).

There was a time when troops took the hill upon command. But there is ample evidence that the best generals prefer leadership to dictatorship. Robert E. Lee and Norman Schwartzkopf, for example, were extremely capable generals who were both humane and firm in their style of leadership.

The day is gone when employees "take the hill." Now the employees may ask, "Why? Who wants the hill anyway?" They might reply, "If you want the hill, you take it." Or, "We'd like to discuss the pros and cons of taking the hill. We've got other things to do today."

If shuttle diplomacy cannot be combined with the skills of most supervisors, neither does the traditional marine-sergeant approach work. The employee feels put down by the supervisor and resists more firmly, denying or minimizing the problem. Leslie says, "It (coming late) hasn't been that often anyway," and in a similar way, Leslie resists by asking, "Why are you picking on me? Are you calling in the others to talk to them, too?"

Then, concluding that fighting back would not work, Leslie tried another ploy—that of lukewarm compliance.

Leslie will doubtlessly make a half-hearted effort to comply with the company policy for a brief time. But much of his/her energy will be expended upon nursing resentment toward management.

Because of the supervisor's lack of understanding, the worker often gets even with a fury—in passive or even in active ways, making it obvious that this style of management does not work.

But tyrannical boss management should be abandoned for personal reasons as well. It is not to your personal advantage to act like a totalitarian ruler. The Center for the Study of Disease Control estimated that lifestyle accounts for a high percentage of deaths in several categories.

Heart Disease	54%
Cancer	37%
Stroke	50%

If smoking, drinking, overeating, and lack of exercise can contribute to the constriction of veins and arteries, how much more does a rigid and harsh attitude contribute to a deterioration of health?

Consequently, the despotic style of management should be abandoned not only because it is counter-productive from the employees' point of view, but for an equally important reason. It doesn't work, and it can only lead to more frustration, anger, and resentment toward the manager.

In summary, you must ask yourself what this form of management does to your disposition, your emotions, your stomach, your heart, your veins and arteries, and to the rest of your organs? Does this kind of supervision help or hurt you? Isn't it better to assume the role of coach?

The WDEP System: Leslie Once More

There is a third way to deal with Leslie. The Participatory or Democratic Manager seeks to involve the worker in the solution by use of the WDEP System. The supervisor, acting as coach, helps Leslie do the following:

- **W** Determine *Wants*
- **D** Describe what is being *Done*
- **E** *Evaluate* a Specific Behavior and/or wants
- **P** Make a Specific, Realistic *Plan*

I suggest that you pay close attention to how the use of the WDEP System facilitates a focus on the employee, rather than on extraneous issues. This is done in a patient, kind, and direct manner without sarcasm or rancor. This focus keeps the responsibility where it belongs—on Leslie.

It should also be noted that the supervisor chose to deal with one issue: the employee's commitment to be on time. If the session were longer, or extended into other times, other directions could be taken and other issues could be dealt with. At the conclusion of the dialogue, several alternative directions and issues are indicated.

This interview begins in the same manner as in the first two sessions.

Sup.   Leslie, you've been late and have lost other time, too. I know you have a rough time of it. But I need to talk with you about this.

Leslie   I'm sorry. I'll try to do better. Things are extra rough for me lately. I don't know how some people do what I have to do every day.

Sup.   Tell me something. Do you like your job?

Leslie   Yes, but I'm a single parent—on my own with two kids. I have to do it all now. I don't get any help and the kids take advantage of me.

Sup.   I understand that you have a difficult time of it. I'd like to ask you this: are you interested in moving up—getting a promotion?

Leslie   Yes, I'd like that very much. I'm trying to work hard. But I have a lot to cope with. Like today, I had to wake Sue about five times...

Sup.   Leslie, you're a good worker. Your work is accurate and prompt and you get along with the other employees. These are important qualities for anyone who wants a promotion, and you have them.

Leslie   I try.

Sup.   I want you to stay here at this company and I'd like to see you get a promotion.

Leslie   That's good to hear.

Sup.   In other words, you want me to be on your side when it comes to promotion?

Leslie   Yes, I sure do! Are you telling me you're unhappy with me?

Sup.   I'm saying that it would be difficult for me to go to bat for you with your record of lateness. But for my part, I want to be on your side.

Leslie   You want to help me get a promotion?

Sup.   Yes, your work is good. The problem is with the time lost. Do you have any idea how much it is?

Leslie   I'm not sure. I don't think it's a very big deal.

Sup.   (Showing her a paper) Here is a record of your hours. Tell me what you see as you read it.

Leslie   It looks like I've been late five times this month, for a total of more than two hours, and that I've had to leave three times, for a total of another 2.5 hours. The total is 4.5 hours.

Sup.   What do you think about that?

Leslie   It's a lot, but I do work hard.

Sup.   You work very hard, Leslie. That's why I asked you about whether you want to move up in the company. But my question is, what is your judgment? What conclusions do you come to when you see that record?

Leslie   It's a fair amount of time.

Sup.   It's more than five hours a month—if you only miss another half-hour this month. Multiply that by 12 and we have 60 hours a year.

Leslie   That's 1.5 weeks a year!

Sup.   Does that sound like something the company wants to live with?

Leslie   I see what you mean.

Sup.   I want to be on your side when promotion time rolls around. Is coming late going to make it easy for me to do that?

Leslie   It sure won't!

Sup.   To put it another way, what effect will your lost time—60 hours a year—have on your promotion?

Leslie   Well...it won't help me get it.

Sup.   What can I tell management today if they ask me about you? I can't lie to them.

Leslie   I see what you mean. This tardiness is a real problem. It's *not* helping me.

Sup.	You are absolutely right. It won't help you get a promotion. Let's say there is one promotion available and you and another equally capable employee, who is prompt and has no lost time, are in the running. Who will get it?
Leslie	I sure won't.
Sup.	What about the effect on others when you come late and leave early?
Leslie	They don't say much, but they don't like it.
Sup.	What happens to the work when you miss 60 hours each year?
Leslie	It slows down. Others have to do it.
Sup.	Can you do something about the problem?
Leslie	I guess so.
Sup.	I'm not clear. Is that "yes" a firm "Yes?"
Leslie	It's a firm "Yes."
Sup.	What will you do this week?
Leslie	I'll try.
Sup.	I know you'll "try," but will you do it?
Leslie	All right, all right. I'll be here every day.
Sup.	All day?
Leslie	Yes—on time and all day.
Sup.	What will you have to do in order to be here on time and stay all day?
Leslie	I'll have to figure out how to change the morning routine and schedule appointments differently—maybe on Saturday. But I hate to give up my Saturday…
Sup.	What about that promotion, and what about making it easy for me to recommend you?
Leslie	I see your point. To get promoted, I'll must change.
Sup.	Change by taking the responsibility to figure out how to manage your time; make a better schedule.

Leslie   I can do it. I'll really be here—on time—and stay all day.

Sup.   How about committing yourself to it for one week?

Leslie   Sounds good.

Sup.   Leslie, I want to be able to recommend you, to have a congenial atmosphere in the office, and to get the job done. And I appreciate your willingness to work on this. Let's talk in a week—same time, same day.

In this case, the supervisor helped Leslie define the goal—to get a promotion. This was followed by helping Leslie evaluate the current behavior of coming late and losing other time from the job. The criteria for evaluation are:

**What is the effect of what you are doing
on what you want?**

It hurts the chances of getting a promotion.

**What is the effect of what you are doing
on other people?**

The co-workers don't like it.

**What is the effect of what you are doing
on the work itself?**

The work slows down.

**What is the effect of what you are doing
on management?**

They are less than thrilled.

Finally, a realistic, attainable plan is made. The supervisor does not settle for "I'll try." Rather, the supervisor elicits a firm commitment to the plan. In short, the supervisor used the WDEP System...

- **W** Determine *Wants*
- **D** Describe what is being *Done*
- **E** *Evaluate* a Specific Behavior and/or Wants
- **P** Make a Specific, Realistic *Plan*

It was stated earlier that the Supervisor could proceed in other directions during the interview and deal with other issues which might include the following examples.

1. A review of Leslie's successes and specific projects that were completed in a timely and accurate manner.
2. Helping Leslie plan more specifically the morning routine in order to arrive early.
3. Describing in detail exactly what will need to happen to Leslie's work habits in order to get a promotion.

You are invited to describe other directions and issues you would like to discuss with Leslie.

4. _____

_____

5. _____

_____

6. _____

_____

7. _____

_____

8. _____

_____

The purpose of the dialogue between Leslie and the supervisor is to illustrate the WDEP System. It should not be seen as a totally exhaustive session which is final. There are other avenues that could be explored and perhaps more facts to uncover which would provide data for more interview sessions.

Nevertheless, the supervisor has made an effort to insure that Leslie perceives the problem as being his/her own, and that this conference is the formulation of a strategy for solving the problem. This will lead to a solution that involves both parties. This Participatory Manager approach is thus made practical and operational through communication with employees via the WDEP System.

Chapter Eight

Thinking You Can Manage in an Instant

One-minute rewards and reprimands can be useful, but they hardly take the place of a detailed conference in which the manager tries to motivate the employee to work harder and smarter. The danger in our high-tech, push-button society is to delude ourselves into thinking that people will change if the manager merely pushes a reward or punishment button. Even if this were true, it would still be necessary to find the right button. This takes conversation, communication and conferences. The WDEP System provides structure, organization, and direction for this process.

In the example of Lee, it becomes clear that such rewards and reprimands are only the beginning—and of themselves are insufficient. Lee has worked for the company for five years. Though once energetic, dependable, and thorough, the quality of Lee's work has diminished. Negativism, listlessness, lack of attention to detail, and failure to follow through are now characteristics of Lee's work.

The Manager tries the quick-fix approach.

Mgr. Lee, you've been sliding the last few months. Do you agree?

Lee No, I think I'm the same as I've always been.

Mgr. But look at these numbers. You were producing ten widgets. Now it's seven. That's not acceptable. Can you increase it to ten again?

Lee I didn't know it was that bad.

Mgr. It's bad. But I know it can be better. I've seen you do better in the past.

Lee Well, okay. This is going to be hard.

Mgr. You can do it—I know you can. Two years ago, you were at twelve. Ten are within your reach, and I know you'll want to stretch out and do your best.

Such a session with an employee is not harmful; it may be helpful for a few. Moreover, in the quick-fix above, the manager is direct and does not put the employee down, but rather praises Lee. *The mistake is that the manager thinks this is the best solution for most employees.* It should be only the beginning of further communication.

The WDEP System

As in the case of Leslie, there is a better way to deal with Lee—using the WDEP System. An example follows.

Mgr.   Lee, when I called you in to talk today, what went through your mind?

Lee   I figured I was in trouble.

Mgr.   Yes, in a way, and I want to talk to you about it.

Lee   What have I done?

Mgr.   It's not what you've done, but what you've not been doing that's on my mind. First I want to share my viewpoint with you. You don't seem to be as happy as you once were. Lately, you seem to be more listless and distracted.

Lee   I guess you're right. I feel really bored with the job. Sometimes, I think I'm on a treadmill. It's the same thing day after day. I come in to work, go over the same kind of projects, check the figures, make recommendations that a kid could make, and then go on to the next proposal.

Mgr.   I appreciate you for being so straightforward with me. It's not easy to continue to do a job if it feels like drudgery. Let's talk more about that point in a few minutes. First, tell me what happened on the ABC Contract last week.

Lee   I didn't get the data from the sales department. I don't know what's wrong with them. They didn't send it. And the accounting department really messed up. When I tried to tie the information together, I discovered that the numbers from the accounting department were wrong. I had to rush at the end and there were mistakes in the final version. There really wasn't enough time to get it done accurately.

Mgr.   What had you done to get the information on time?

Lee   I told the sales department to give it to me.

Mgr.   Then what?

Lee   I waited for them to send it.

Mgr.   What about the accounting department?

Lee	They know to send me the figures. They just didn't do it. So I waited.
Mgr.	I'm here to help fix the problem, not fix the blame. And so I want to ask you—did waiting for the two departments help *you* get your job done?
Lee	But it's their job to get me the information.
Mgr.	I know it is. But is waiting passively for them to do their job helping you to function at your fullest capacity?
Lee	No, I guess not. I should have gone after the information.
Mgr.	So next time, what will you do that is different?
Lee	I guess I need to be more involved. I need to ask them to get it to me.
Mgr.	Can you make a plan to do that?
Lee	Yes, of course.
Mgr.	What would such a plan look like?
Lee	Well, it's simple. I'll call them and ask them to send me the information.
Mgr.	Is that enough?
Lee	I guess it should be written.
Mgr.	Sure. Don't make a big deal of it. A memo, a reminder is all you need. When will you do it?
Lee	I suppose it should be done as soon as I get the proposal.
Mgr.	Any other details in the plan?
Lee	What do you mean?
Mgr.	Like telling them how soon you would like the information. Maybe you could say when you plan on working on the proposal and when you need to have it in contractual form.
Lee	I see what you mean. I need to be more thorough and not assume they will stick to a deadline.

Mgr.	Right. Will you follow this plan?
Lee	Yes.
Mgr.	I have a more basic concern that I alluded to before. The ABC Contract is just the symptom. My concern is your overall approach to your job and to your career. Where are you going in your career? Do you have an idea about your general direction?
Lee	I don't know. It's hard to decide where I want to go.
Mgr.	You say "decide." It almost sounds as if you are uncertain about what you want to do.
Lee	I think that's right.
Mgr.	What about your interest in the job? Any thoughts?
Lee	Well, I guess it's boring.
Mgr.	I wonder whether this lack of interest in the job is rooted in uncertainty about where you want to go in your career.
Lee	They are tied together.
Mgr.	In other words, if you are unsure about where you're going, it's hard to get excited or even interested in the details which you encounter on this trip. It's like being lost in a strange city—it's hard to get excited about the scenery.
Lee	Yes, that's it exactly.
Mgr.	How satisfying to you is your "direction" and your job? What do you think as you sit here—now at this moment?
Lee	It's not satisfying at all. It's no longer fun.
Mgr.	Would you like to turn things around for yourself?
Lee	I've not thought much about it. I just figured the job is going to be a bore.
Mgr.	What if it could be interesting? What if you could find a sense of direction and set some goals? I'd like you to think about it. Would you be willing to give

some thought to things like your direction? Where is your present direction taking you? In other words, if you continue to be bored, where will you end up in a year—or five years?

Lee   I've given almost no thought to that.

Mgr.   That's not all. I want to ask you a more fundamental question. Do you really want to work here?

Lee   I'm not sure. Sometimes I think I need a change.

Mgr.   It might be something to think about. For the good of the company, I'd like for you to change your work habits and stay. But let's face it. Maybe the best thing for you would be a change in jobs. Changing jobs is quite common. But I want to emphasize—I'd like you to stay.

Lee   I appreciate your support.

Mgr.   Would you give some thought to these two ideas? "Do I really want to work here?" and "Where am I headed with my current work habits and attitudes?"

Lee   Yes, I'll think long and hard about them.

Once again, it is important to keep in mind that this dialogue is representative of the essential elements of the WDEP System. It is devoid of the usual meandering within most daily conversation. The purpose of these omissions is to present, in as brief a space as possible, the WDEP System to you—the busy manager.

In this summarized session, the manager attempted to get below the surface problem—the ABC Company proposal —to the underlying ennui which may be characteristic of more than one of your employees. Questions and data revealed by the questioning is summarized as follows.

Do you *Want* to work here?

Lee will think about this.
Manager shares his/her wants regarding Lee.

What are you *Doing*?
(Where is your current direction taking you?)

Lee is unsure about this.

Does it help you to wait for the other departments
to provide information? (*Evaluation*)

Lee decides it is not.

What's your *Plan*?

Send memo—think about important questions.

There are other implicit evaluative questions asked in the dialogue. See if you can identify them.

_____

_____

_____

_____

The significant point is that the *Want* component contains more than asking the employees about their wants. It also includes the *Want* of management. A manager using the WDEP System *never* needs to fear losing authority. It is quite responsible, helpful, and sometimes necessary for the manager to reveal to the employee what management wants from him/her.

Thus, the WDEP System not only allows for praise and confrontation, it also provides a vehicle for helping employees look at themselves in an honest, straightforward, and sometimes painful way. And it provides the manager a way to relate to the employee in a direct, non-abrasive manner.

Chapter Nine

Ignoring the Problem

Do you have an employee who is like a piece of furniture or a potted plant? This question does not imply a putdown for such an employee. But it does reflect how you might be dealing with someone. This person is tolerated and, for whatever reason, will never be fired. You know it. The employee knows it. Upper management knows it. Everyone knows that this person is untouchable. And perhaps the problem is not even severe enough to warrant termination. But there seems to be no sufficient carrot or stick to stimulate performance improvement.

The person could be similar to Fran who is two years away from retirement. Most of the workers view Fran as "semi-retired" on the job. Fran usually arrives on time and leaves exactly at quitting time. There is little fear that Fran will need rehabilitation for workaholism! It seems to take a major amount of his/her energy to merely arrive in the morning and leave at the end of the day. Most of Fran's conversation revolves around retirement and how inept the present leadership is—they do things so differently from the way things were done in the 1950s! This criticism is unbridled, and Fran's negativism is vented in front of the younger employees. Everyone knows Fran joined the company at the same time as the original founders and was once a much harder worker.

Fran is so negative and predictable that he/she is rarely engaged by a manager in any serious manner, but is treated like a table or chair around whom everyone walks without noticing. Thus, there is no dialogue like that described below. Who would want to talk to a table or a plant? But the following dialogue is an example of how a manager might engage Fran in a motivational conference—using the WDEP System.

Mgr.	Hello Fran, how are you today?
Fran	Tired...stayed up to watch the movie.
Mgr.	That's exactly what I wanted to talk to you about.
Fran	The movie? Did you watch it?
Mgr.	No. I wanted to ask you about the amount of energy you've been giving the job.
Fran	I do my job! I've worked here twice as long as you!
Mgr.	That's right and I've learned a lot from you. But I want to talk to you about how you're doing now.

Fran   Well as I said, I do my job.

Mgr.   And you're looking forward to retirement?

Fran   You bet! I've got two more years.

Mgr.   Fran, how would you compare your work habits in the last few weeks with how you worked 20 years ago—when you were moving up in the company?

Fran   They're probably about the same! What's the big deal?

Mgr.   Let's be specific. Remember the report I returned to you?

Fran   You mean the one where you said I made too many mistakes?

Mgr.   That's a good example. How did it compare with the reports you did years ago?

Fran   I know what you're going to say. I'm not giving much to the company. But I've paid my dues and I do my job.

Mgr.   Let's stick with the report. What about it?

Fran   You seemed to think it was sloppy.

Mgr.   If it had been a retirement contract describing your benefits, what would you think?

Fran   (Silence...)

Mgr.   What would you do?

Fran   I guess I'd send it back.

Mgr.   Why?

Fran   Because it contained mistakes. I suppose it wasn't too great.

Mgr.   Tell me, how did it compare with what you would have done 20 years ago?

Fran   It was sloppier. That's what you want me to say, isn't it?

Mgr.   I want you to make a judgment on it; evaluate how you did; to take a serious look at what's happening.

Fran   I hate to admit it, but it definitely wasn't up to what I can do.

Mgr.   What happens when anybody's report is not up to par?

Fran   It has to be re-done.

Mgr.   Okay. Now Fran, I'd like to ask you some questions and ask you to look at a broader issue that I've been concerned about.

Fran   Okay. I guess this is my day.

Mgr.   What effect does it have on the younger workers when you turn in sloppy, incomplete, or late work—or when you arrive a half-hour late in the mornings?

Fran   They don't say anything.

Mgr.   But what effect does it have?

Fran   I never thought much about it.

Mgr.   Well, think about it now. What do you guess they think about it?

Fran   They probably think, "If someone else can get away with it, why can't I?"

Mgr.   Exactly! Deep down inside, Fran, do you want them to learn that from you?

Fran   Well, no. But they don't really understand what we went through in the early days.

Mgr.   Is the way you act now and what you say now helping them appreciate it?

Fran   I guess not.

Mgr.   What would help them appreciate the difficulty of the old days and your contribution to the company?

Fran   Maybe if what I do and say now were in line with the traditions and goals of the company, it would help.

Mgr.   We'll come back to that. I have another "deep down" question. Fran, do you think you are working as hard as you can?

Fran   Well...not really. But I've already given 28 years to this company.

Mgr.   I know that, and I'm not trying to minimize it. In fact, I'd like to ask—what kind of worker do you want to be for the last two years?

Fran   I guess it's only fair to work hard. I make a good salary.

Mgr.   That's true. And the pay you got this month is for this month's work—not what you did 20 years ago.

Fran   That's right. We can't rest on past successes, or we will go out of business. I realize that. And as we both know, those young people don't appreciate the past glories of this company or the blood and sweat that went into it.

Mgr.   That's right. They only think about the present. But our jobs depend on the present too. Also, speaking of the younger workers, I'm wondering this: what do you want people to say when you retire?

Fran   Some will be glad to see me go.

Mgr.   Is that the way you want it to be?

Fran   No, I'd like them to think of me as a good worker.

Mgr.   The younger ones will remember the last two years more than the first twenty-eight.

Fran   You're right about that.

Mgr.   And Fran, there's another more important element in all of this—not just what others say.

Fran   You mean what I say? Is that what is most important?

Mgr.   Right. What do you want to be able to say about yourself? "I coasted to retirement, loafing the last two years, and I was a poor example for the younger workers?"

Fran   Hell No! That sounds awful. Is that what you think of me?

Mgr.	I'm definitely afraid it could happen. What do you want to be able to say when you retire?
Fran	"I worked hard up to the end and was an example to the younger workers."
Mgr.	You sound like you mean that. So are you convinced that you could serve as an example to the younger workers? Would you like to be proud of yourself and know that others were proud they knew you and worked with you?
Fran	Yes. Of course I would.
Mgr.	What effect will resting on the past and slacking off have on that goal.
Fran	It can't help.
Mgr.	I couldn't agree more.
Fran	I guess I needed this kick.
Mgr.	I'd call it a gentle nudge. I have a lot of respect for you. You were here in the beginning and you've contributed a lot to me. I don't want to hear negative things about a person of your stature and experience.
Fran	Thanks. I appreciate that.
Mgr.	I see you as a potential influence for good or ill in this office. It's your choice as to how you'll work and what you'll be for the next two years.
Fran	I guess you're right.
Mgr.	Fran, could you reverse your present trend...really give it 100% for one week?
Fran	Sure. I could do that.
Mgr.	How, specifically, would you do it?
Fran	I could stop complaining from now on. I could get here on time. I could stop bad-mouthing new ideas. I know that really irks you at meetings.
Mgr.	You've noticed!
Fran	I sure have.

Mgr.   Could you commit yourself to a realistic, attainable plan?

Fran   For how long?

Mgr.   Let's try one week and then talk again.

Fran   Sure, I can handle that.

Mgr.   I'd like to add one more idea.

Fran   Sure.

Mgr.   Could you not only refrain from complaining, but could you say something positive about the company —maybe two or three times a day? Like telling someone why you chose to stay here rather than go elsewhere when you had the opportunity? This would be a positive plan rather than a negative one—to stop complaining. They're both good ideas, however.

Fran   I could do that.

Mgr.   Let's talk again in a week. Okay?

Fran   Okay. And thanks a lot.

This case, like the others, contains the heart of the WDEP System. The effective use of the WDEP System does not eliminate all "side bars of conversation," but it does serve to lessen and abridge them so that the interview can truly be motivational.

In the session with Fran, the following elements of the WDEP system were used with accompanying results:

What do you *Want* the younger employees to say about you and how do you *Want* them to perceive you?

Favorably—not as a burned-out, pre-retiree.

What did you *Do*, re: the report?

Did it sloppily.

Evaluate the result of the sloppy report.

It has to be re-done.

Evaluate the impact of negativism on others and on you.

It does not help.

What *Plan* will you make?

Speak positively about the company; stop griping.

Once again, the manager used the practical, down-to-earth, efficient WDEP System. Nevertheless, other directions could be pursued and more detail could be discussed with Fran. Such efforts might include the following.

1. Exploring in more detail how Fran will handle the next two years.

2. Allowing Fran to describe how the office and the job could be better. Frequently, the complainer has many helpful ideas that are ignored.

3. Helping Fran set some goals (*Wants*) to work on for the short term and for the next two years.

You are invited to write several other directions and issues which you could explore with Fran.

_____

_____

_____

As in the previous cases the manager has been direct and to the point, but has shunned the autocratic approach. On the contrary, the Participatory Management style has become operational by helping the employee...

- Identify **Wants**
- Describe what he/she is **Doing**
- **Evaluate** the effectiveness of behavior
- Make a **Plan** of action.

...and that is the heart of the WDEP System.

Chapter Ten

Getting Defensive,
Making Excuses,
and Attacking

Getting defensive, making excuses, and attacking are mistakes made by all managers at one time or another. One of the most explosive and difficult situations is when someone is denied a promotion and demands an explanation. If more than one person was truly qualified, the winner might be only slightly more qualified—and perhaps in a non-quantifiable way. The following dialogue occurred when Lynn was denied a promotion and initiated a conference.

Mgr.   Lynn, you wanted to see me?

Lynn   You're damn right, and you know why. This is the second time I was passed over for a promotion and I want to know why. Why did Lou get the promotion instead of me? I've worked my butt off for this company and I get nothing for it.

Mgr. I didn't make the decision. But I did the best I could. Lou's been here longer and that's that. I don't see anything to discuss.

Lynn Lou's only been here one month longer than me.

Mgr. I didn't say how much longer. Besides, Lou's got more experience than you in that field.

Lynn Wrong again! I've worked on those projects more than Lou. You're the one who assigned them to me. This is just one more unfair way I've been treated by this company—and especially by you.

Mgr. Maybe my criteria are wrong. You'll be the first one to be considered next time.

Lynn Is that a promise?

Mgr. Of course.

Lynn I don't believe your promises. You've said things like that before and they never come true. It's so damn unfair, and you've not given me much of an explanation about why I didn't get it. I want to know why I didn't get the promotion. All you've given me are flimsy cop-outs.

Mgr. I'm not the one who decides. It's upper management that really selects the people for promotions.

Lynn But you recommend, don't you?

Mgr. ...Yes, I do.

Lynn Who did you recommend?

Mgr. I'd rather not say. It's sort of confidential.

Lynn That's the old management shuffle. Another cop-out! I'm sick of it.

Mgr. (Angrily) You know Lynn, I'm really tired of your

nit-picking and constant griping. All I ever get from you are complaints. You never offer anything constructive. I can't do anything right in your eyes. Sometimes I wonder why you stay. I guess you enjoy making life miserable for all of us!

Lynn   That's an awful thing to say. I can see I'll never get promoted by you. If I were in the union and not salaried, you'd hear more about this.

Mgr.   Well, I'm sorry I blew up. I didn't mean what I said.

Lynn   It's too late to apologize. Now I know how you really feel about me. I'll never get a promotion as long as I'm under you. I was absolutely right. You do have it in for me!

Mgr.   No, I don't.

Lynn   Forget it, I gotta go.

Mgr.   Me too. Good-bye!

In the above dialogue, the manager was uncomfortable and wanted Lynn to be agreeable. The manager also seemed unsure about how to handle such a situation. The defense of "the secret method for promoting" was feeble, and then when asked about the recommendation, the manager copped out—as Lynn bluntly observed. This Laissez-faire approach did not work. It only seemed to intensify Lynn's anger and resentment. This, in turn, provoked the manager who lost control, quickly making it evident that beneath the veneer of "nice guy" was the behavior of an Authoritarian Manager.

The above case is brief and is intended to illustrate various kinds of mistakes in a short space. Still, it portrays statements that are frequently made in managerial sessions.

The WDEP System

The next dialogue illustrates a rather subtle application of the WDEP System to this very difficult situation.

Mgr.   Lynn, you wanted to see me?

Lynn   You're damn right. And you know why. This is the second time I was passed over, and I want to know why Lou got the promotion and I didn't. I've worked my butt off for this company and I get nothing for it.

Mgr.   I can see you are upset about this and I don't blame you. It might be good for you to get some things off your chest. I'd be willing to listen.

Lynn   It's just that I've been here as long as Lou and I've done more difficult work at times. And sometimes I think you have it in for me.

Mgr.   Lynn, I know your qualifications, and I know you think I have it in for you, but I look at it differently. In my mind, I want the best for the company.

Lynn   Then, why didn't I get the promotion?

Mgr.   Even if I would tell you all the deliberations that went into this decision, which I won't do, would it really satisfy you? Do you honestly think you would then agree?

Lynn   Probably not.

Mgr.   It seems to me that what you really want is the pro-motion—not just a reason why you didn't get it.

Lynn   That's true. It just seems so wrong that Lou was picked over me.

Mgr.   I don't blame you for being upset. But I want to ask you this. Is there anything at all that I could say now that would totally remove your anger...that would really satisfy you?

Lynn   I would only be happy if I had the promotion.

Mgr.   That's what I think too. I can say this. The way it works is that I submit names and make a recommendation. I recommended Lou and I'm not going into all the details with you. Upper management made the final decision.

Lynn   At least you're honest even though you won't say much about it.

Mgr.   There's an important question to deal with here. It seems to me that you have two choices between now and the next series of promotions in six months.

Lynn   What do you mean?

Mgr.   You can either nurse the resentment, grumble, make it worse, and spread it around, or you can keep it for a while, then let it go, work hard with a positive attitude, and look toward the next promotion time.

Lynn   I'm just so frustrated.

Mgr.   And angry too. So which choice is to your best advantage?

Lynn   I see what you mean. If I work hard again, will I be promoted in six months?

Mgr.   I make no guarantees. It will be up to you to convince me to recommend you. From my point of view, I want to see you move up. But I want to see everyone move up. If you succeed in convincing me, you'll get the recommendation.

Lynn   In other words, it's up to me?

Mgr.   It's up to you to perform to a degree that I can recommend you. That's the way the system works.

Lynn   I get it.

Mgr.   I have another question. If you let this disappointment get you down and tear you down further, what will be the outcome?

Lynn   I'll probably not get anywhere next time a promotion is open.

Mgr. That's right. Spreading dissension is not going to be to your best advantage. And also, what is the effect on you personally?

Lynn I'll just be miserable for a long time.

Mgr. So will it help you to nurse your hurt and disappointment?

Lynn It can't help me in any way whatsoever.

Mgr. I agree. In other words, if you bounce back, your name will be in the hat in six months and you'll feel better inside.

Lynn I'm going to look to the future. I still don't agree with your decision, but you're the boss. But I'm still upset.

Mgr. There's one more thing. How long will you hang on to this anger and resentment? A month? A week?

Lynn That's a strange question. Since you caused it, maybe you could tell me.

Mgr. I don't look at what I did as *causing* your anger. But I don't want to argue the point. One thing for sure— you can either nurse the anger or try to let it go. It's where you go from here that is most important to me and to the company—and I hope to you too. So how long...?

Lynn I don't know. I'd like to get rid of it now.

Mgr. That's hard to do. Why don't you leave just part of it here now. Keep some of it for a while.

Lynn Okay, but for how long?

Mgr. That's up to you.

Lynn This is weird. But maybe I'll be over it in a week.

Mgr. That sounds good. I wouldn't expect you or anyone else to get over such a disappointment quickly. But maybe in a week you could cut it loose—or at least cut it down a little.

Lynn Okay. One week will do it.

Interpretations and Suggestions

Before reading further, you are invited to describe your interpretations of what happened in this dialogue and to indicate suggestions for future discussions.

The applications of the WDEP System are more indirect in this case. The following guidelines will help you if you keep them in mind as you conduct conferences with the Lynns in your organization.

1. *Accept the fact that the employee is going to be angry and resentful for a while.* You cannot remove the anger, but you can help them choose to lessen the effects.

The dialogue with Lynn is a succinct version of what might require two or three fifteen-minute sessions spread over a week.

2. *Stand your ground and don't apologize.* Explain how the decision was made, but don't go into endless detail about it. A brief explanation is all Lynn is capable of hearing at this time.

If you fight Lynn and take a self-justifying or belligerent stand, as did the manager in the first dialogue, you will find the employee resisting and rebelling more firmly. Paradoxically, if you let your sail down, the wind will lessen.

3. *Take responsibility for your own actions.* If it is your decision, don't cop out by blaming others. Be honest and straightforward. But keep confidential that which should not be disclosed.

The employee might not agree with this, or accept your position immediately, but after the heat of the moment disappears, he/she is more likely to be cooperative.

4. *Ask the employee if there is anything you could say that would totally satisfy him/her now.* This diffuses some of the anger and helps show that the employee is attempting to put you on the defensive. This subtle form of *Evaluation* is an indirect way of asking people what could help make them feel better.

In fact, Lynn does not want an explanation. The promotion itself is still the primary *want* for Lynn, and even if you were able to reverse the decision and bestow the promotion, Lynn could still feel some resentment that the promotion was only awarded after a storm of protest.

5. *Help the employee Evaluate and Plan future behavior.* How will resentment be dealt with in the future?

Ask employees what is best for them emotionally. What is best for them regarding the next promotion, and what is best for the people around them? Lynn was asked if nursing the anger would be advantageous. It might take longer than a brief interview for the Lynns in your company or organization to relinquish resentment and anger at not being promoted. But by using the WDEP System, you have succeeded in very clearly communicating the following things.

a)   You are still the manager.

b)   You will take responsibility for your decision.

c)   You won't be intimidated, controlled, or manipulated into rash statements by their anger.

d)   You believe that their feelings of anger and disappointment can be temporary. They can change them for the better.

6. *Don't make any promises about the future.* If employees cut loose the resentment, they will have a better chance of having their names in the hat for future promotions. Even then, however, there is no guarantee that they are assured of promotion. Communicate this clearly, calmly, and unambiguously.

They will respect you for this straightforwardness and for the strength you show by taking this position. They will also realize that no promotion is automatic.

7. *Remember, the employee is upset.* In the heat of the moment, employees may say things that they will regret later. There is no need to join them in regrettable statements, and there is no need to hold their spur-of-the-moment, out-of-control behavior against them. Allow them to save face and remember the saying, "Only amateurs hold grudges."

8. *Help the employee Plan how to deal with the resentment.* Lynn decided it would last a week, and then be cut loose. This is the culmination of the WDEP System—a plan of action. It frequently does not require much dialogue, especially if the *Evaluation* has preceded it.

9. *Help the employee make a Plan to rectify any work-related behaviors that need to be changed* (in order to be considered for future promotions). This was not discussed in the session with Lynn. The supervisor dealt with the immediate and most obvious part of Lynn's behavior—the resentment, disappointment, and anger. The plan for change in work-related behaviors is most aptly handled when the employee has settled down and is more open to this type of planning.

The session with the good worker who has been turned down for a promotion is one of the most difficult to conduct. You might have sympathy for the employee, and believe that a promotion is well-deserved. You might even get upset when you are accused of "unfairness" or "copping-out." You are tempted to fight fire with fire. But that is always a poor choice. Fight fire with water. The WDEP System can be the water that is used to quench the fire of resentment, anger, revenge, and retaliation. It can help the worker look to the future with a positive and realistic plan.

Chapter Eleven

Avoiding the Problem Behavior...
or Initiating Plans for Change

Dale is a good worker and is bright, humorous, energetic, and ambitious. But Dale doesn't always take the work seriously and also has problems getting along with co-workers. Dale "carries the load," seeing others as unwilling to bear their share of the work. Besides constantly complaining, Dale spreads rumors and is often a back-biter.

Moreover, it is unknown for Dale to admit to mistakes—they are always someone else's fault. Being right about every political, social, and personal issue is Dale's hallmark. Regarding job-related matters, Dale is omniscient, infallible, and all but clairvoyant! Others, however, fail to see these virtues. Their description includes such traits as arrogant and infantile—a person who projects blame on others, never admitting responsibility for a problem. Another problem has surfaced recently—an offensive body odor which is more than a little noticeable to other workers.

Most recently, Dale and another employee, Wilson, had a loud argument during which both engaged in cursing, accusations and name-calling. This occurred in the presence of several suppliers who brought it to the attention of the department manager.

In this dialogue, the manager reluctantly tries to discuss the problems with Dale.

Mgr.   Hello, Dale. How are you today?

Dale   Fine. I'm glad to get a chance to see you today. Those two people I work with aren't pulling their load, and I'd like you to do something about it.

Mgr.   What do you mean?

Dale   I have to do half their work. Like the other day when that XYZ job was late. I got it out with very little help from my two co-workers.

Mgr.   What else is wrong? Weren't you late today?

Dale   We car pool it, and I was late today because I was working at home and lost track of the time.

Mgr.   Weren't you supposed to have that work done yesterday?

Dale   Yes, but the Art Department didn't give me the layout on time.

Mgr.   Did you tell them you needed the layout?

Dale   Nobody told me I needed it until yesterday.

Mgr.   Yesterday, what was the argument with Wilson about?

Dale   Wilson started it, and I'm tired of the stuff I have to take from him.

Mgr.   Dale, you're the problem. You act like a jerk. I'm tired of you. You have to get serious about your job. And I've heard about some other things you need to change.

Dale   I've heard those rumors. They're not true.

Mgr.   Another thing, everyone knows you play a lot of sports.

Dale   So what? I play on weekends.

Mgr.   Well, people talk about this—even during the week.

Dale   It doesn't interfere with my work.

Mgr.   Okay. I just thought you ought to know.

Dale   Know what?

Mgr.   Look, I have another appointment. I have to go.

In the above dialogue, the manager is guilty of some of the same behaviors that the employee uses. It is as though the manager imitates Dale's angry behavior. This manager then gets angry, resorts to innuendo, and finally just avoids the uncomfortable topic of body odor. The problems are left hanging and unsettled.

The WDEP System

While it is only human and quite understandable for the manager to avoid dealing with a difficult employee who is irresponsible or who has an embarrassing problem, it is crucial that the issues be discussed as expeditiously as possible. Unaddressed problems such as these rarely get better on their own. In fact, they nearly always get worse.

On the next page, a different kind of conference is described. This is a real motivational session with Dale in which the manager utilizes the WDEP System.

Mgr.	Hello, Dale. How are you today?
Dale	Fine. I'm glad I got a chance to see you today. Those two people I work with aren't pulling their load, and I'd like you to do something about it.
Mgr.	That's exactly what I want to discuss with you.
Dale	It's about time. I've told you about this before.
Mgr.	I want to talk to you about how you are handling the situation.
Dale	What do you mean?
Mgr.	I want to center our discussion on you, not on other people.
Dale	I got no problems.
Mgr.	Here's an example of what I want to talk about: the argument you and Wilson had yesterday.
Dale	It was Wilson's fault.
Mgr.	I'm not concerned about whose fault it is. There were three suppliers within earshot, and two of them told me about this argument.
Dale	It was Wilson's fault. Are you going to talk to Wilson, too?
Mgr.	Right now, I'm talking to you and I want to ask you about your actions.
Dale	I'm doing just fine.
Mgr.	In some ways you are doing well. Right now, I want to discuss how you can improve.
Dale	I don't see anything wrong.
Mgr.	I do. And I want you to look at yourself and what's happening. I want to discuss only one point—how you and Wilson get along. It seems to me there is a major problem between you two.
Dale	Wilson brings it on.
Mgr.	Then maybe you're the one who will need to solve it. What have you been doing that didn't help? For

instance—what happened when you and Wilson had that argument yesterday?

Dale I didn't do anything. Wilson started to jump me and I told him off. I've known him for years. We always talk to each other like that.

Mgr. In other words, you argued loudly with him.

Dale Yeah, like I say, we talk like that all the time. His voice was just as loud as mine was.

Mgr. Let me get this straight. You were yelling at him.

Dale Yes, but...

Mgr. (Interrupting) Did you see the three suppliers about ten feet away from you

Dale Yes there were a lot of people looking at us.

Mgr. What impact does this have on other people—no matter how well you and Wilson know each other?

Dale I never paid much attention.

Mgr. What do you think *now*—at this moment?

Dale I guess it does kinda shock a stranger.

Mgr. I agree and in my opinion, the situation must change. I want you to do some changing—especially in your conversation with Wilson.

Dale But what about Wilson...?

Mgr. (Interrupting) What about you?

Dale Well, I guess it did get a little out of hand. I guess I could try to do better.

Mgr. Dale, you've been with us for four years. I've known you that long, and I'd like to say something sort of blunt to you.

Dale OK. Fire away.

Mgr. When you talk about other people and their faults, you are very clear and definitive. But when I asked you about yourself, you used the word "guess" twice and the word "try" once—in a single sentence. You sound very tentative about taking responsibility for your own behavior.

Dale   I sorta see what you mean.

Mgr.   "Sorta?"

Dale   Yeah, I need to be more committed. Is that what you're saying?

Mgr.   Do you think that attitude would help you or hurt you? Would it help the other people around you or would it hurt them?

Dale   I guess it would help. I'll try to do better.

Mgr.   It will take more than trying. It will take action and a firm commitment. I know you can get along better, and I'm going to hold you to a plan. Can you make a plan to get along with Wilson?

Dale   Yes, I'll do that.

Mgr.   How will we measure the success of your plan?

Dale   I don't know.

Mgr.   Will you listen to a suggestion?

Dale   Do I have a choice?

Mgr.   It's usually not wise to ignore the manager's advice in such a crisis.

Dale   Okay, okay.

Mgr.   When you disagree with Wilson, keep your voice low. That's not asking too much. I'm not even asking you to be buddies—only to keep your voice low when you disagree.

Dale   I can handle that.

Mgr.   How committed are you? Is that a "maybe?" Is it an "I guess," or "I'll try," or an "I'll do what I can?" How about something more firm?

Dale   It's a firm promise. I will do it.

Mgr.   Sounds good. We'll talk about it again. I do have one more item for you. I don't know why, but I've noticed a strong odor about you several times. I don't like to bring it up, but if I had this problem, I'd appreciate it if someone told me.

Dale   Sometimes I'm in a hurry in the mornings, and I play sports on the weekends.

Mgr.   You work close to people, often looking at the same drafts and drawings. I think it is important to consider their feelings. Will you do whatever it takes to be presentable?

Dale   Yes, I'll take care of it.

In this session, the manager used the WDEP System in a direct, almost confrontational manner. But noticeably absent was any hint of criticism or any degrading comments. The manager was direct, but not unkind.

The manager stressed the *Doing* aspect of the WDEP System, but this dialogue also illustrates the *Want* aspect—how the manager sees the situation and what is wanted from Dale—"I want you to look at yourself and at what's happening." The manager is clear about what is wanted—especially in Dale's future conversations with Wilson. It is as though the manager holds a mirror before Dale and asks him/her to look at the behaviors and evaluate them.

Thus, the manager played a very directive role in helping Dale *Evaluate* current behavior. Each of Dale's behaviors could be handled in a similar manner. While the evaluation must ultimately be internalized by the employees, it does not need to originate with them. The manager can initiate the *Evaluation*, and can even suggest a *Plan* of action.

Finally, this dialogue illustrates a further aspect of the System—eliciting a higher level of commitment. "I'll try" is not as firm as "I will."

Other Directions

As in the other cases, the manager could have explored other avenues. I suggest you reflect on previous cases in this book and glean from them other aspects of the WDEP System that could be applied. Summarize them below.

_____

_____

_____

_____

_____

_____

_____

Chapter Twelve

Confronting an Unhealthy Lifestyle

Company ABC conducts health screens each year for all employees. Readings on cholesterol levels, blood pressure, and weight are obtained. All employees are then interviewed by the Life Style Coordinator, who reviews the health screen and "counsels" them for a few minutes.

Thus, this case is intended to provide an effective way for company nurses, life-style coordinators, or other medical personnel to deal with managers, supervisors, and all employees whose health indicators show that the direction in which they are moving is not helpful. The details will become clear in the dialogue.

LSC   Good morning, Jody. How are you today?

Jody   In a hurry. How long will this take?

LSC   Are you rushed today? Maybe we could schedule this when you have more time.

Jody   I'm always rushed, and I never really have time for you to tell me what I already know. Let's do it now. Today is as good or bad as any other day.

LSC   We have your health screen. And it doesn't look very good.

Jody   I figured so. Give me the bad news.

LSC   Your cholesterol is 280. Your blood pressure is up —180 over 95—and your weight is up ten pounds from last year when it was eight pounds more than the year before.

Jody   I knew you were going to tell me this. But I have a very hard time on the job and at home. My spouse isn't much help with the kids. And I have to travel so much—staying in hotels, eating at odd hours when I'm starved after working a twelve-hour day. Things are getting ahead of me. I feel like my life is out of control.

LSC   I think you'd better get your blood pressure down and your weight, too—as well as that cholesterol.

Jody   You don't know the pressures I have! And it's not easy to eat right when you travel so much and sit in a motel room at night.

LSC   But you've gained eighteen pounds in two years, and everything else is higher too. It's time you do something about this, or you're going to have a serious problem.

Jody   I'll tell you something else. My staff here has been cut, and now I'm doing some of their work. There's no end to this frustration and pressure, and now you tell me this. It's just one more project I have to work on.

LSC   You really need to relax and exercise more. Why don't you get some relaxation tapes to listen to at night, and then go to the company health center and get on an exercise program? They can help you. You ought to be concerned about your weight, cholesterol, and blood pressure. It won't get any better if you don't do something about it.

Jody   All right, all right. I'll change my diet, go to the gym, and get some tapes.

LSC   I'm going to record your decision in my notes.

Jody   Now that's important, isn't it!

LSC   Yes. We are required to document these sessions. If I can be of any further help, please let me know.

Jody   Oh, I will. Good-bye.

LSC   Good-bye, and good luck with your program.

The LSC did not do a bad job of counseling Jody. Concern and professionalism were demonstrated and factual information was provided—three elements that are central to the delivery of human services. But there is a fourth component that was missing—the skill for bringing the concern, professionalism, and factual information to the employee in a meaningful way that leads to a specific action being planned and carried out. The WDEP System provides this skill.

The WDEP System

As in the cases of Leslie, Lee, Fran, Lynn, and Dale, there is an alternative way that can be used to help Jody examine *Wants*, *Evaluate* what is being *Done*, and make specific, attainable *Plans*. As in the other cases, the art of asking questions is illustrated in the dialogue which follows.

LSC   Good morning, Jody. How are you today?

Jody   In a hurry. How long will this take?

LSC   Are you rushed today? Maybe we could schedule this when you have more time.

Jody   I'm always rushed and really don't have time for you to tell me what I already know. Let's just do it now.

LSC   Sounds good. It should take less than a half hour. Can you commit to being here for about 20 minutes and going over some important information? I'll need you to be fully present while we do this.

Jody   Okay, but I think I know the bad news.

LSC   Well, there's bad news, but more importantly, there is also good news. First tell me how the job is going. I ask because job, family, and really all aspects of life, are connected to our health condition.

Jody   My job is very hard. I travel a lot, work 12 hours a day when I'm on the road, don't get to eat until I'm starved, and spend the few remaining minutes watching TV in the motel room. Sometimes, I don't sleep too well at night because I eat late. And of course, I'm still smoking. Then, when I go home, I don't get much help from my spouse either. I guess I'm a mess! Do you agree?

LSC   I don't believe you are a mess. The way I see it is that you are a dedicated worker, spouse, and parent. I'd like to see that continue. But I do have an idea that by changing a few things, you could feel better.

Jody   I don't think I can add any more to my busy life.

LSC   I didn't say "add." The word I used was "change." But let's come back to that later.

Jody   Oh, you want to give me the bad news? I think I know what's on the health screen.

LSC   Before I do, I want you to think about this, not as bad news, but rather as signals. The items on the health screen are like the lights on the dashboard of the car. They serve a purpose, don't they?

Jody   You're right. When they go on, they tell the driver that something needs attention.

LSC   I like how you put that. Same way with your body, which is read by the health screen. Our bodies send us signals and the health screen is a reading of the signals. So there is bad news for you. But there is also good news. The good news is that you can do something about the problem.

Jody   Can I see the numbers?

LSC   Here they are. Tell me, what do you see?

Jody   It's pretty much what I thought. Cholesterol—280. That's up from 260 the year before. My blood pressure isn't any lower and my weight it up 19 pounds over the last two years. Put that together with my smoking, and I'm a walking time bomb!

LSC   That's the bad news. But it's also good news. Your body has sent you a very clear warning signal.

Jody   (Meekly) I guess it has.

LSC   What do you think your body is saying to you?

Jody   You used the word "change." But that's hard to do.

LSC   How urgent is the signal? Is your body saying, "Jody, it's no big deal. Just smoke one pack instead of two, and exercise by getting off the plane and running through the airport?"

Jody   You have such a way of putting things!

LSC   Thanks. But what do you think about the message?

Jody   It's telling me to make a serious turn around, or else it will stop me permanently.

LSC   You have a good way of putting things too. That could well be the message.

Jody   I guess I need to do something.

LSC	Let me ask you some questions. What could you do in the next week that could hurt you?
Jody	Keep going the way I am.
LSC	Like what?
Jody	Smoke and rush around.
LSC	What about exercise?
Jody	Oh yes. I could sit around in the evenings and eat while I watch TV.
LSC	Do you want to turn things around, get the cholesterol down, lower your weight, feel better, watch your kids grow up, and enjoy life more?
Jody	What can I say?
LSC	I know it sounds like an obvious question. But your real answer is important.
Jody	Yes, of course it is.
LSC	How much do you want to do this?
Jody	I really need to.
LSC	Is this a weak whim which you'll forget or a firm commitment?
Jody	If I'm to be alive for a long time, I'd better be firmly committed.
LSC	I agree. It will take some effort. But it will be a different kind of effort from the mad rushing and scurrying around that you've become accustomed to.
Jody	When do I start with this project?
LSC	Where do you want to start?
Jody	When I used to exercise, I always felt good.
LSC	Would you go to the company health center and set up a program? It's fun—and never overwhelming.
Jody	I can get down there in a week or so to set it up.
LSC	How about calling now, on my phone, to set up an appointment at the earliest possible time?

Jody   Might as well. You know, I heard that you try to get people moving on these things right away.

LSC   Well my mother used to tell me, "There's no time like the present."

Jody   (Makes call and sets appointment.)

LSC   How about the smoking cessation program here? Have you ever been to it?

Jody   No, I haven't.

LSC   Is not going helping or hurting your effort to quit?

Jody   I get the idea. Can I use your phone again?

LSC   No problem!

Jody   (Makes call and sets appointment.)

LSC   I think you have a start. There are other things to get involved with, but that is enough for now.

Jody   You want to tell me about my weight?

LSC   Not now. I think you know the situation. Maybe we can deal more specifically with it at another time. Just ask yourself when you eat, "Is this selection helping me or hurting me?"

Jody   It will be a reminder to me.

LSC   Could you return in two weeks to talk? I would like to talk to you once more about your overall stress. I know some other ways to reduce it.

Jody   I'd like that.

LSC   Meanwhile, you have a plan. Are you firmly committed to the two appointments?

Jody   Yes I am.

LSC   See you in two weeks. Same time?

Jody   Amen!

In the above dialogue, the Life Style Coordinator used the WDEP System to help Jody identify the *Wants* regarding unhealthy behaviors and elicited a commitment to change. The plan was not intended to be a grandiose strategy that would address every aspect of Jody's life. Rather, it was intended to be a realistic beginning. There could be a temptation to push Jody to make an inflated plan which would be desirable, but unattainable. Then, with failure, guilt feelings would increase and the cycle of stress would be intensified.

***

A brief exercise follows in which you are asked to describe how the LSC accomplished the various goals in the session. To get you started, the first two are answered. Please refer back to the dialogue if necessary.

1. LSC got Jody's full attention.
   Asked Jody explicitly for 20 minutes. Jody's full attention was needed.

2. Presented data from health screen.
   Showed it to Jody and asked what Jody saw.

3. Helped Jody feel less stress about the "bad news."

   _____

   _____

4. Used concrete images to show importance of data.

   _____

   _____

5. Asked Jody about his/her wants.

_____

_____

6. Had Jody evaluate specific behaviors.

_____

_____

7. Asked about the direction of Jody's life.

_____

_____

8. Helped Jody make a *realistic* Plan.

_____

_____

9. Helped Jody make an *immediate* Plan.

_____

_____

10. Provided for follow-up.

_____

_____

Other Directions

As in all cases in this book, other directions could be taken by the LSC. Perhaps more discussion could be given to the weight problem or the generalized stress which Jody felt. Below are several questions which end this chapter. These can be used for discussion or to stimulate your own private thinking.

1. Why did the LSC choose to emphasize the plan for exercise and smoking?

2. Why didn't the LSC choose to emphasize weight control for Jody?

3. Should this employee be referred for more intensive counseling? Why or why not?

4. How would you have used the WDEP System if Jody had become more hostile toward you as LSC?

5. When you see Jody in two weeks, what will you explore with him/her? What will be your goals?

Chapter Thirteen

Improving Overall Quality

Imagine a newly-hired Chief Executive Officer of the EFG Company, who brings a philosophy different from that of many people presently in the corporation. The new CEO is interested in increasing the quality of the company's product. However, this manager wants to get away from the current thinking that short-term financial gains are necessary to satisfy stockholders and upper management.

That undesirable mind-set is widespread among the management team. Group meetings have been held to try to introduce change. The manager has asked them to think about a few ideas for increasing the excellence of the company—such as improving inter-departmental cooperation, removing fear as a motivator, and increasing teamwork.

The CEO is now following up the group meetings with an individual session with one of EFG's vice-presidents.

CEO I called you in so we could talk more about our meeting the other day in which we discussed how to raise our overall quality. Have you had any after-thoughts since that meeting?

VP I really like the ideas that were emphasized. I don't think we can do everything fast, but I think we need to do something—especially in the area of teamwork.

CEO I definitely agree. If we focused on just one aspect, such as teamwork, we might increase the job satisfaction of our people and then reduce their anxiety about job security. How do the managers feel about their own job security?

VP They think that since you were hired from outside, many of them will have to quickly look elsewhere for jobs. One repeated the old saying, "A new broom sweeps clean."

CEO What does that perception do to the overall quality?

VP It can't help. It's probably very destructive. Too much time is lost just by talking about rumors.

CEO I've given them reassurance. But they'll only be convinced when they see action.

VP That's true. They're still shaky.

CEO You made a point at the meeting about teamwork that seems to point toward a solution. If people feel good about each other and their work, many problems will be solved.

VP That's what came out of the meeting. And yes, I did say that. It also seems to represent a consensus from what the others said.

CEO That message was loud and clear. What would help our people feel they are part of the team?

VP   They need to feel that they are contributing to the organization and that their best is good enough. I think we need to have more performance reviews for our people.

CEO   How would that help?

VP   They would know someone cares about their work; that we're trying to increase their quality.

CEO   Here's a question for you. What does an employee think about when he or she goes in for a review?

VP   They probably think, "How did I do?"

CEO   That's my guess, too. But what's lacking in that question?

VP   I think I see what's behind your question. In the context of teamwork, emphasizing the "I" might not be helpful.

CEO   Even if individual persons reach their own goals, the company might not be reaching its goals.

VP   They might also be hesitant to set very high goals for themselves because, in order to look good, it's only necessary to do a little better than they did before.

CEO   We need to improve the system as a whole.

VP   What can I do to accomplish this?

CEO   What can *who* do?

VP   I see what you mean. It needs to be a team effort—even at our level!

CEO   What will be the effect of the team approach at the level of upper management?

VP   If we do it, it will show that we believe in it, and others will take it seriously, too.

CEO   We can't ask others to do something we don't do.

VP   Is that why you started with a group meeting rather than seeing us one on one?

CEO   Exactly.

VP   So, we need to set up group sessions in each unit.

CEO   That's down the road. What do we need to do even before that?

VP   I think we'd better start with upper management, and go through the process ourselves.

CEO   What would we talk about?

VP   If we're to improve overall quality, we need to discuss customer needs.

CEO   I wonder if we would agree about what they are.

VP   Probably not, but we'd better give it a try.

CEO   There's another important possibility. We may have one perception of customer needs, but others might have different ideas.

VP   We need to get input from all levels. I'm beginning to see how this might work.

CEO   That topic is only the beginning. After we've defined customer needs, what else do we need to talk about?

VP   We need to figure out how to improve our operation.

CEO   So as we do this, I think that one of the results will be better teamwork.

VP   Right! The feeling of teamwork is really a side-effect of an improved process for meeting customer needs.

CEO   And what happens to the workers' fears and anxiety— and the short-term results for the stockholders?

VP   Worker's fears will lessen. But I don't know about the pressure to get the short-term quarterly results.

CEO   We'll have that urgency with us for a long time. We haven't solved everything—only taken a step.

VP   There's something different about this entire process.

CEO   When you meet with the groups, ask them to try to identify what is different. Ask them how they feel about it. But I have one suggestion: hold your own opinion till the end.

VP   Good idea! I like the idea about talking about the process rather than individual people.

CEO   What happened to the performance reviews?

VP   Oh yes. What did happen?

CEO   Well, how do they fit into this discussion?

VP   If we emphasize the process and all the elements described in the books you mentioned at the meeting, we won't need them.

CEO   Eventually we won't. But we want to help everyone perceive the program and its goals in their entirety.

VP   Right. If they just think that performance reviews are being discontinued, they will miss the point completely. This is really an effort to increase our ability to meet customer needs with a better process. A small part of that includes replacing performance reviews with process thinking.

CEO   Do you think it will help or hurt to bring up performance reviews at this point?

VP   Originally I thought it was a good idea, but it is incidental to the entire process. Let's not get into it yet.

CEO   What are the next crucial steps?

VP   I think we need to have upper management meet to discuss customer needs and how to improve our ability to meet them. Then, have other levels and units do the same.

CEO   What about those age-old walls between departments?

VP   They'll need to develop teamwork, also. Eliminating turf wars won't be easy.

CEO   But we can at least make a dent. How would you think that could be done?

VP   They need to talk to each other more.

CEO   I agree. Could you draw up an overall plan for getting this system in gear?

VP	Sure. When do you want it?
CEO	Tomorrow at noon.
VP	Tomorrow? This might take a while.
CEO	Not if it's only one side of a page and is just an outline of the overall process.
VP	In other words, I should stay away from the content of the meetings except for the general categories we spoke about.
CEO	Right. It will just be a working paper that we might change as a result of the meetings with upper management and with other levels.
VP	So, we're imposing very little on them.
CEO	The only thing I want to impose on them is the high standard of quality which I'll figure out after I have all their input. I've seen all the statistical data. My job is to establish levels of quality, not delegate it. But I want input, even for that decision, from as many people as possible.
VP	I'll have the outline on your desk early tomorrow morning. Could we talk for a few minutes then?
CEO	That's the idea. I'll be here—just stop in.

In this session, the CEO used the WDEP System to incorporate some of the concepts of W. Edwards Deming in a very rudimentary way. (This is not intended to be a comprehensive treatment of the work of Deming. To understand his monumental contribution, the reader is advised to consult his work and that of his followers.) This session is a demonstration which shows how the WDEP System can be used in even the highest levels of management. On any level, people can be motivated, with the use of these principles.

In the previous dialogue, the CEO addressed the following issues:

1. Developed with the VP a structure for allowing employees to define their wants, provide input, and examine the company's effort to meet customer needs.
2. Asked the VP to evaluate his own perceptions and those of the employees. This was done in a non-critical and non-demeaning manner.
3. Encouraged the VP to take initial action for implementation—to prepare and present a brief outline to the CEO the next day.

Other Directions

As in all the cases in this book, the manager (CEO) could pursue other directions in this or following sessions. Some are listed below. You are invited to list your own ideas regarding directions that you think this (or any) CEO could follow in such a session.

1. Deal with stockholder desire for quarterly increases.
2. Be more specific regarding the content of the meetings.
3. Discuss in more detail concepts such as Inputs, Processing Systems, Outcomes, etc.

4. _____

   _____

5. _____

_____

6. _____

_____

7. _____

_____

Chapter Fourteen

Conclusion

Now that you have read this book in its entirety, you have had some exposure to the WDEP System. And although you might not feel like a superstar, you should generally understand how to use these principles. I encourage you to think about the following ideas:

- You can change your life by using the WDEP System at work and with yourself. Though it requires hard work and determination, the system is applicable to your own wants and behavior as well as to those of your employees.

- You can help your children by using it with them. You supervise them, and they choose many of the same behaviors that employees choose. The WDEP System is an excellent parenting method.

• You now have a structure which is usable in all communication with other people. You never need to get bogged down in excuses or criticism. You have a workable alternative to the Authoritarian and Laissez-faire Managerial Styles.

***

Besides all of the above ideas, I suggest that you *put into action* the following strategies:

1. Begin immediately!
   Don't waste a minute!
   Start today!

2. Begin by using the principles with employees whom you find it easy to deal with. When you achieve immediate success, you can easily build on it—making you feel more confident to begin working with employees who are more difficult.

3. Make a plan to use the ideas at home with your children. Teach them to define what they **Want.** Ask them to **Evaluate** what they are **Doing**, and help them make **Plans** for changing their behavior in order to get what they want. When your children learn the art of evaluating their own behavior, you will be surprised at how easy parenting can be.

4. Recognize that these ideas are easier to understand than to put into practice. The dialogues in this book are simplified summaries, designed only to teach the principles of the WDEP System. They should be adapted to your personal style of communication.

5. Realize that you can always improve. If you continue to use the WDEP System, you will be more skilled in six months than you are now—*so start now.*

6. Recognize that human behavior is a choice. There are some workers who will choose destructive behaviors and disregard your best efforts to offer help. You can extend a hand to them, using the WDEP System, but you cannot *make* them change.

***

Finally, I want to reemphasize that the most beneficial application of these principles is in your own life. If you begin to define your **Wants,** look at what you are **Doing, Evaluate** the attainability of your *Wants* and how your actions are helping or hindering you, and then make **Plans** for your own improvement, you will open doors of opportunity that you never knew existed. Write down your goals and wants for the next six months—and then for one year. Review them each day by examining how your behavior is helping you get there. Then make a daily plan to fulfill your dreams.

Annotated Bibliography

I have purposely limited this annotated bibliography. The list of truly valuable management books is endless, with many helpful resources available in any bookstore or library. This list contains some of my favorites. Needless to say, it also contains some which I have authored.

Curwin, Richard and Mendler, Allen. *Discipline with Dignity.* Alexandria, Virginia: Association for Supervision and Curriculum Development, 1988.

This resource describes how to have effective discipline. It includes appropriate use of consequences.

Deming, W. Edwards. *The New Economics, 2nd Ed.* Cambridge, Massachusetts: Massachusetts Institute of Technology, 1993.

This book represents many of Dr. Deming's final thoughts about quality, education, and the future in general.

Glasser, William. *Both-Win Management.* Los Angeles: Institute for Control Theory, Reality Therapy, and Quality Management, 1980.

A book about how management and labor can work together to attain ends that are agreeable to both.

Glasser, William. *Control Theory.* New York: HarperCollins, 1986.

A good summary of motivational theory. We are all motivated to fulfill needs that are born in us. Our behavior is a choice, and we can change it to better fulfill our needs.

Glasser, William. *Control Theory Manager*. New York: Harper–Collins, 1994.

An explanation of the theory of control theory as it applies to the world of work. Contains general guidelines for becoming a lead manager.

Wubbolding, Robert. *A Set of Directions for Putting (and Keeping) Yourself Together*. Cincinnati: Center for Reality Therapy, 1991.

This book contains practical suggestions for taking better control of your life, for feeling better, and for relating to others in a healthy manner.

Wubbolding, Robert. *Understanding Reality Therapy*. New York: HarperCollins, 1991.

An easy to read explanation of needs, wants, behavior, perception and other ideas. It includes anecdotes, metaphors, humorous stories.

Wubbolding, Robert. *Using Reality Therapy*. New York: Harper-Collins, 1988.

A book on how to deal with people. It contains ideas for adapting this method to business in a no-nonsense, down-to-earth manner.

Ziglar, Zig. *Over the Top*. Nashville, Tennessee: Thomas Nelson, Inc., 1995.

This book has on-target advice for tapping inner motivation; written, in my opinion, by the world's greatest motivational speaker.

Index of Cases

Specific Components of the System	Illustrative Cases (specific chapters)
Exploring Supervisor Wants	*Leslie (7), Fran (9), Lynn (10), Jody (12)*
Sharing Wants	*Lee (8), Fran (9), Dale (11)*
Exploring Perceptions	*Lee (8), Fran (9)*
Sharing Perceptions	*Lynn (10), Jody (12)*
Getting a Commitment	*Leslie (7), Fran (9), Dale (11)*
Determine Overall Direction	*Lee (8), Fran (9), Jody (12)*
Focus on Specific Action	*Fran (9), Lynn (10), Jody (12)*
Attainability of Wants	*Lynn (10)*
Impact of Behavior on Others	*Leslie (7), Fran (9)*
Effect of Work to be Done	*Leslie (7), Fran (9)*
Helpfulness of Perceptions	*Jody (12)*
Effect of Behavior on Wants	*Jody (12)*
Specific Action Steps	*All Chapters*

About the Author

Dr. Robert Wubbolding is the Director of Training and a Senior Faculty Member of the Institute for Control Theory, Reality Therapy, and Quality Management in Los Angeles. He is also Professor of Counseling at Xavier University where he has taught people who deal with nearly every type of employee and client—in companies, schools, probation and police departments, recovery programs, churches, etc.

In addition to over 100 publications, Dr. Wubbolding is the author of seven books including: *A Set of Directions for Putting Yourself Together*, *Using Reality Therapy*, and *Understanding Reality Therapy*. These books comprise a major contribution to the discipline of Reality Therapy, as well as a summary of Control Theory, a theory of brain functioning which explains human motivation.

He is internationally known, having presented programs throughout North America, Asia, the Middle East, and Europe. He has served as consultant to drug and alcohol abuse programs for the U.S. Army and Air Force. He was a group counselor at Talbert Halfway House for Women Ex-offenders and has served as elementary and secondary school counselor, and a teacher in Adult Basic Education. He has been a consultant to the Management Institute of the University of Wisconsin where he taught Effective Management Skills. Dr. Wubbolding is a Psychologist and Nationally Certified Counselor.

For more information, contact:

The Center for Reality Therapy
7672 Montgomery Rd.
Cincinnati, OH   45236
Telephone   (513) 561-1911   Fax   (513) 561-3568